U.S. ARMY DIAMOND T VEHICLES IN WORLD WAR II

CASEMATE | ILLUSTRATED | SPECIAL

CASEMATE | ILLUSTRATED | SPECIAL

U.S. ARMY DIAMOND T VEHICLES IN WORLD WAR II

DIDIER ANDRES

CISS0012

Published in the United States of America and Great Britain in 2022 by
CASEMATE PUBLISHERS
1950 Lawrence Road, Havertown, PA 19083, USA
and
The Old Music Hall, 106–108 Cowley Road, Oxford OX4 1JE, UK

This book is published in cooperation with, and under license from, Sophia Histoire & Collections. Originally published in French as *Les Véhicules Diamond T de l'US Army* by Didier Andres © Histoire & Collections 2021
English edition © 2022 Casemate Publishers

Hardback Edition: ISBN 978-1-63624-160-9
Digital Edition: ISBN 978-1-63624-161-6

A CIP record for this book is available from the British Library

Design by Myriam Bell
Translated by Alan McKay

Printed and bound in the Czech Republic by FINIDR s.r.o.

For a complete list of Casemate titles, please contact:

CASEMATE PUBLISHERS (US)
Telephone (610) 853-9131
Fax (610) 853-9146
Email: casemate@casematepublishers.com
www.casematepublishers.com

CASEMATE PUBLISHERS (UK)
Telephone (01865) 241249
Email: casemate-uk@casematepublishers.co.uk
www.casematepublishers.co.uk

Contents

Introduction

The story of the company with the diamond, founded in 1905 and called the Diamond T Motor Car Company, is closely linked to one exceptional man, Charles Arthur Tilt.

Charles Tilt was born on June 28, 1877 to Canadian parents, Joseph E. Tilt (b. 1842) and Sarah Bowes (b. 1854). In 1875, the family immigrated to the U.S. and settled in Illinois in 1878. As the heir to a rich shoe industrialist, Charles Tilt made good use of the family firm's reputation, going so far as to borrow the advertising symbol created for his father's company products. This showed the letter T, the first letter of the family name, inside a geometrical shape displaying a diamond. The prodigal son built his first motorized vehicle in 1905 but it was not until two years later that regular car production really began, with three models in the catalog.

1911 was the year in which the first big change occurred in the new Diamond T Company. Responding to a special request from a customer, Charles Arthur Tilt built his first truck.

He was quick to realize that this was a commercial niche where there was room to grow, since the world

Left: Called the Wrecker Truck No. 1, this Diamond T from the late 1920s was classified in the 10-ton, 6x4 category. It carried a bridging structure with manual handling only that could easily lift the little 1927-Model Chevrolet that has been modified as a telephone-line-laying vehicle. (U.S. Army SC-100920)

PARTS LIST
U. S. ARMY
Class-"B" Liberty Trucks
ALL REPAIR PARTS FURNISHED BY
HIGHWAY SERVICE CORPORATION
INDIANAPOLIS, INDIANA

Above and right: Assembling liberty trucks was the first partnership between the U.S. Army and the Diamond T Motor Car Company. Some 638 trucks of this type were assembled by the Chicago firm. These pictured here are garrisoned in the U.S. (Private Collection)

of private automobiles was in the hands of the big manufacturers like Ford where competition was tough and profit margins small.

The Diamond T Motor Car Company's best year for civilian truck production was 1936, a 12-month period in which 8,750 trucks were registered. During the firm's 53 years' existence, it is generally agreed that around a quarter of a million trucks came off its production lines.

The first military production was during World War I with the Diamond T Motor Car Company being one of 15 companies assembling the Liberty 4x2, 3-ton Class B trucks. Out of the 9,452 built, 638 came from the Chicago workshops in 1917/18.

In the mid-1930s, Diamond T became one of the Army's official suppliers. But it was not until 1940 that orders for the brand new 6x6, 4-ton trucks began rolling in: some 36,500 were supplied between November 1940 and August 1945, proving that the Chicago company had indisputably asserted itself in the sector. On September 19, 1956, Charles Arthur Tilt died after spending more than a half-century at the head of his company.

The postwar period was difficult for the automobile industry and in particular for the Tilt family. In 1958, the White Motor Corporation swallowed up Diamond T which became a subsidiary, but this wasn't enough to save the company. In 1967, White merged its Diamond T branch with that of Reo, bought up in 1954, to form Diamond T-Reo Truck Inc. In doing so, the last vestiges of the Diamond T Motor Car Company disappeared after 62 years' existence. In 1975, Diamond T-Reo Truck Inc. was declared bankrupt and its assets sold off. Subsequently, the Swedish company Volvo bought the White assets and with the various buyoffs, today holds the rights to the brand names of three American vehicle builders.

Top: Diamond T Dump Model C from 1934, a 4x2, 1½-ton truck used by the Corps of Engineers. The vehicle was powered by a 4,311-cc, six-cylinder Hercules JXB engine, rated at 68 bhp at 2,100 rpm. (U.S. Army SC-114443)

Middle: 1st Cavalry (Mecz), Fort Riley, September 6, 1939. The wrecker was powered by a six-cylinder, 7,015-cc Hercules YXC engine, rated at 93 bhp at 2,300 rpm. The axles were made by Timken and the main four-speed gearbox as well as the transfer case by Brown-Lipe. (U.S. Army SC-100924)

Right: On September 14, 1939 at Fort Belvoir, the 5th Engineer Regiment tested roadblocking techniques. A simple roll of barbed wire stretched out in the middle of the road very quickly stopped any vehicle trying to force its way through. (U.S. Army SC-114442)

1 Where It All Began

One might think, wrongly, that the U.S. Army's mechanization has a long history that began in the early 20th century. Although it is true that the need for motorized vehicles exploded because of World War I, progress slowed right down during the interwar period.

It was not until 1939 that the auto industry could start supplying vehicles again. The Army was authorized to start buying vehicles originating directly from civilian production through invitations to tender, and could impose on suppliers changes in some features such as radiator and headlight protection, and towing hooks.

The only characteristic that could not be changed was the payload. A list of five categories was published and on it, alongside the ½-, 1½-, 2½-, and 7½-ton categories, was one that proved providential for the Army: the 4-ton, 6x6 truck.

Left: In the race to obtain Army orders, the White Motor Company received notice to produce 85 vehicles with contract W-398-QM-7509 and registration numbers USA-W-00287 to USA-W-00292 for six of them, with the designation Cargo Wrecker. The others bore registration numbers in the USA-W-412873 to USA-W-412951 series as simple cargo trucks, the 950 x 6 Model trucks. (White Motor Co.)

Below: The 5th Infantry Division on winter maneuvers, Fort Custer, Michigan, February 1941. With registration number USA-W-412900, this White 950 x 6 Model truck was one of 79 6x6, 4-ton cargo trucks (Cargo Trucks, 6x6, 4-ton, in military parlance) which the Army ordered in 1940 from the Toledo firm. (Associated Press photo, ref.: 23190)

Each order, be it for a particular unit or for personnel use, had to be made through an invitation to tender, the order going to the lowest bidder. Three orders were placed at the beginning of 1940 under such conditions, with three separate companies.

For the same type of 4-ton, 6x6 vehicle, the Army received three different vehicles, as follows: eight made by Ward LaFrance Truck Division of Great American Industries Inc., 11 by Autocar Co., and 85 by the White Motor Co., although the only difference requested was the fitting, or not, of a winch.

This gave rise to two different designations: Cargo and Cargo/Wrecker. In the military jargon of the period, the qualification Cargo/Wrecker did not mean a vehicle equipped with a hoist, but merely a breakdown truck used as a field workshop.

When war broke out in Europe, the Senate changed the rules of the game and authorized the Army to make use of negotiated contracts. New orders for 4-ton, 6x6 trucks were placed after tests and comparisons, and strangely enough it was a fourth player who was to reap the benefits, the Diamond T Motor Car Company.

When, at the end of 1940, it was a matter of agreeing a contract using the new negotiating procedure for 22 cargo/wreckers and 388 cargo trucks, all with winches,

Above and Right: Coming directly from civilian production, the 950 x 6 Model proudly sports the White grille behind that added protection for the radiator and headlights. As they also had to take on the role of prime movers, the vehicles had two spare wheels, both installed on the front axle alongside the normal wheel to increase traction. (White Motor Co.)

Below: The eight vehicles supplied by Ward LaFrance Truck Corporation were Model 106s, part of contract no. W-398-QM-7748 (USA-W-412981, USA-W-482639, USA-W-00949 to USA-W-00951, and USA-W-00953 to USA-W-00955). They all had a cargo body. (Private Collection)

Below right and bottom: In U.S. Army nomenclature, the registration numbers beginning with a double zero designated vehicles for special use. In the 1940/1 rolls, it is quite usual to find normal trucks registered like this and designated as cargo/wrecker trucks (Trucks Cargo/Wrecker in military parlance) which actually made them breakdown vehicles. This "00" prefix was to be found again with the cargo vehicles, for example the GMC CCKWK-353 trucks ordered (18 examples delivered) and the Dodge WC-5, -12, and -14 trucks (596 delivered). These did not carry handling equipment, but were delivered to the units as field workshops. (Private Collection)

Left; Even though there was no open talk of war as yet in the States, great strides were made in standardization, which only intensified in subsequent years. The tarpaulins, wheels, and even the heavy metal cargo bodies were already similar and common to the various builders who avidly shared the meager 1939/40 orders. (Private Collection)

various other manufacturers turned up, but not Ward LaFrance which withdrew, whilst Reo Motors Inc. presented a rather sketchy, unfinished prototype.

On the other hand, Diamond T had carefully studied the market and its competitors' vehicles. It sold its Model 967 truck to the Quartermaster Corps, and the Autocar C-7066, the White 950 x 6, and the Ward LaFrance 106 trucks were soon forgotten.

When the United States entered the war, military orders took on a new dimension.

Now that the equipment was satisfactory, the Army was able to modify the orders both for quantities and specifications. It was also freed of all civilian contingencies since the government had requisitioned the car industry for the war effort. This process was set up in mid-1940 but took almost a year to become totally operational.

This first order placed with Diamond T Motor Car Company in this new era, for 6x6, 4-ton trucks, was not an isolated example. The Chicago firm also received

Below; This Ward LaFrance truck, registration no. USA-W-00949, lost its cargo body in favor of the Ernest-Holmes twin lifting jib and thereby became the pre-series vehicle for the future 6x6, 4-ton wreckers. In 1940, still under strict budgetary restrictions, the Quartermaster Corps used all its ingenuity in developing its cartage whilst keeping costs down at the same time. This explains why existing vehicles were used as the bases for new ones. (U.S. Army SC-123889)

orders for some 309 4x2 vehicles of all sizes, just prior to the order for 5,871 12-ton, 6x4 prime mover artillery tractors, and this excluded the thousands of halftracks which came off its production lines.

As far as the 6x6, 4-ton trucks were concerned, the Army placed an order for 34,009 vehicles, of which 2,949 were cancelled, giving an actual production of 31,060 6x6 trucks in this category between 1940 and 1945.

Above and left: The Autocar Model C-7066 truck was the third type of vehicle to be bought and studied with a view to developing the future 6x6, 4-ton range. With only 11 bought—USA-W-00275 to USA-W-00277 and USA-W-410775 to USA-W-410782, or three cargo/wreckers and eight simple cargo trucks—Autocar did not supply too many more vehicles than Ward LaFrance. (U.S. Army Signal Corps)

Opposite: It was with the 104 trucks supplied by White, Ward LaFrance, and Autocar that the Army laid the foundations for its new motorization in the 6x6, 4-ton category. The Field Artillery and the Corps of Engineers were given the task of laying down the protocols for commissioning the trucks, but it was a fourth player who profited from all this experience: Diamond T became the successful, final buyer when the large orders commenced. (U.S. Army Signal Corps)

USA

2

The First Generation

Model 967

At the end of the Army tender process, the Diamond T Motor Car Co. won the bid with its Model 967, on offer for the price of $4,990.

Its rivals were not able to make such a low offer, with the White 950 x 6 at $5,610 and Autocar's C-7066 at $6,140. Unwittingly, the Chicago firm had just won the initial order for what was to become one of the most lucrative markets of World War II as far as medium-tonnage road vehicles were concerned.

In its initial form, contract no. W-398-QM-8270 was based on a requirement for 21 vehicles of the cargo/wrecker type with registrations between USA W-001210 and USA W-0011330, and 388 simple cargo trucks. The Quartermaster Corps very quickly added a further 589 cargo trucks (USA W-417678 to USA W-462751). So, 998 Diamond T Model 967s were ordered in 1940. The Army took the new truck on charge spread over two years, with the first 366 examples at the end of 1940 and the final 632 in 1941.

The first 998 Diamond T 6x6, 4-ton trucks had the builder's designation Model 967; these were the start of a production run consisting of almost 30,000 vehicles in this specific category and were much appreciated by the Army. (U.S. Army Signal Corps)

The Shape

The Diamond Ts were of a traditional design with the engine in the front part under a long hood, a closed-in, more or less centrally placed cabin, and a technical rear part.

These three parts were installed on a chassis formed of two main straight side members, joined by six riveted traverses. It was 256.88 inches (or 21 feet 5 inches) long and 34 inches wide and was made of chrome-vanadium steel. A 15,000-lb Gar Wood 3U-615 winch was fitted to the front part.

Its ⅝-inch-diameter cable was 300 feet long, ending with a chain and hook. The winch worked off the engine, power being transmitted via a PTO shaft with braces through a Gar Wood Model 74Y6000 power takeoff, located on the left-hand side of the gearbox. Controlled by a lever situated inside the cab, this power takeoff had two forward and one reverse gears.

Flexibility, together with a reduction in the effects of the rough road surfaces, was obtained by using a

Assembly line of Diamond T Model 967s at Chicago, Illinois. With their very specific front grille, they could not be confused with other models of the brand. (Diamond T Co.)

composite suspension made up at the front of a set of 12 semi-elliptical leaf springs, two of which were made of chrome-vanadium steel and the other ten chrome-manganese, the whole coupled to Houde Model BBGH hydraulic shock absorbers. At the rear were sets of nine leaf springs made of silicon-manganese steel, each being assisted by four reaction links which ensured that the axial alignment of the sets was correct.

Only the Model 967s had this special front with an unincorporated front grille also covering the headlights. Taken from the workshop manual, TM 10-1603, this shot details the bodywork elements:

1) Cab door handle
2) Grab handle
3 & 9) Rear view mirror
4 & 8) Windshield wiper blade
5 & 7) Wiper arm
6) Tri-master ventilator
10) Hood side
11) Radiator cap
12) Brush guard
13 & 22) Front fender
14 & 18) Headlamp bracket
15) Front bumper
16) Winch assembly
17) Front tow hook
19) Fender step plate
20) Cap nut
21) Front axle drive flange
23) Battery shield
24) Running board
25) Battery shield door
26) Front fender shield assembly

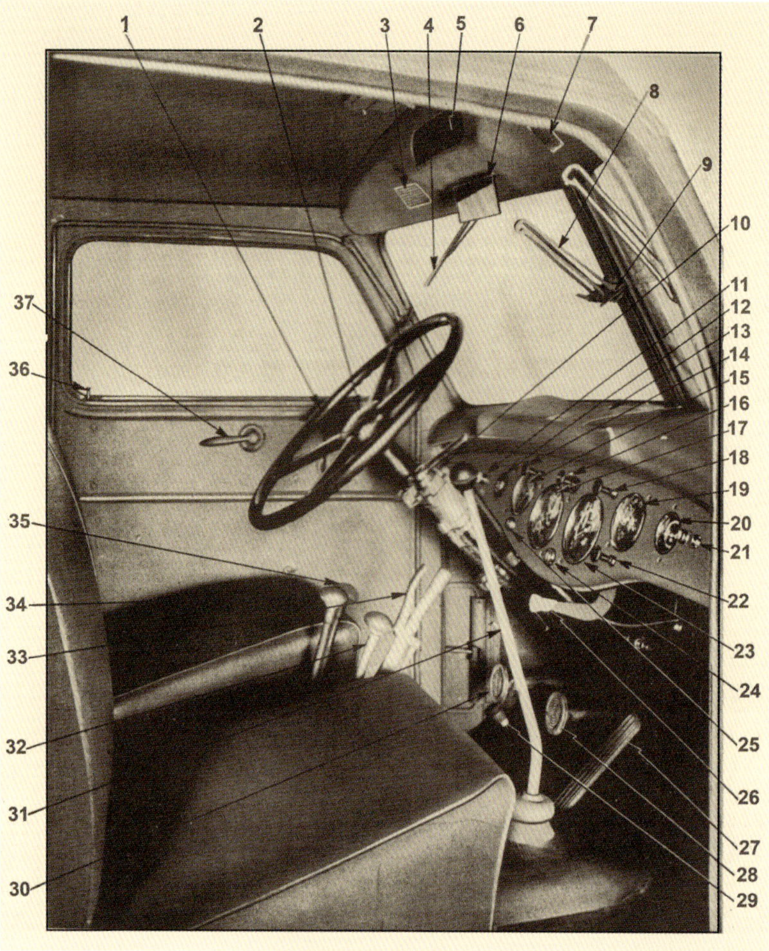

The Mechanics

Using 9.00x20 10-ply tires, the Diamond T 967 was borne by three Timken-Detroit Axle Company differentials. These were of the double reduction type for the two rear axles, reference SFD-153-TW and reference F-2090-TW-74 for the front differential. The vehicle was powered by a Hercules Model RXB gasoline engine, made up of a single block, with space for six cylinders surmounted by a two-piece cylinder

Left: Coming directly from civilian production, the inside of the cab retained the same characteristics:

1) Steering wheel
2) Horn button
3) Warning plate
4) Windshield wiper
5) Glove compartment
6) Rear view mirror
7) Caution plate
8) Windshield sector arm
9) Sector arm thumb screw
10) Hand air valve
11) Windshield wiper control
12) Battery ammeter
13) Winch caution plate & shifting plate
14) Spark control
15) Tachometer
16) Main light switch
17) Instrument cluster
18) Choke button
19) Air pressure gauge
20) Viscometer
21) Windshield wiper control
22) Throttle button
23) Speedometer
24) Ignition switch
25) Tachometer set hand lock
26) Cowl vent control handle
27) Accelerator pedal
28) Brake pedal
29) Dimmer switch
30) Clutch pedal
31) Gear lever
32) Power takeoff shift lever
33) Hand brake lever
34) Declutching lever
35) Transfer box shift lever
36) Night latch button
37) Remote control handle

(Extract from TM 10-1603)

Right: The new 4-ton, 6x6 vehicles were tested in extreme conditions, equipped with chains on all the axles, twin front axle wheels, maximum payload in the cargo body, and weighted-down trailer. (Diamond T Co.)

head. This side-valved 8,211.39-cc (501-cubic-inch) engine was rated at 122 bhp at 2,300 rpm. It was water-cooled using a radiator fitted with 11 pipes and cooling fins, and a water pump located on the left of the engine block. A 22-inch-diameter, six-blade ventilator fan was fitted on the front to increase the cooling of the 36 quarts (34.6 liters) in the cooling circuit.

Transferring engine power was through a Borg & Beck Model 14Q single dry clutch plate and a Clark Model 326-VO-18 gearbox with five forward and one reverse gears, together with a Wisconsin Model T7M3 two-speed reduction transfer box, which was also used to engage the front differential to change the vehicle from 4x6 to 6x6 drive.

With these mechanics, and a Zenith Model IN167J carburetor, an AC Model D pump, and a 40-gallon fuel tank, the Diamond T 967 had a range of between 155 and 200 miles, and a consumption rate between 3.875 and 5 mpg, depending on the type of road surface and the driving conditions.

All the truck's electric equipment worked on 6 volts, from two 6-volt batteries giving 118 amps/hour, linked up in parallel, except for a 12-volt starter for the engine. This difference was made possible thanks to the ignition system's electrical circuit which alone was supplied by the two batteries set up in series, via an electromagnetic contactor. All the electrical components were made by Autolite.

The brake system, which also worked on the trailers, was the compressed-air type, made by the Westinghouse Automotive Air Brake System. It was fed by a two-cylinder compressor, driven by belts from the cooling fans, the compressed air produced being stocked in two cylindrical tanks installed between the side members of the chassis. Quick couplers for the trailer brakes were located at the rear of the vehicle. There was also a set of fixed connections at the front to enable the truck to be coupled to the trailer in the case of breakdown. Exceptionally, they could also be used, though it was not really recommended, for maneuvering a trailer from the front. The parking brake consisted of four sabots and a 14-inch-diameter disc, installed on the transmission shaft, just behind the transfer box.

Above: Fort Benning, March 23, 1942. The 87th Engineer Battalion has loaded its cartage in order to take part in the extensive spring maneuvers. The vehicles are held fast on the railway wagons. (U.S. Army SC-133279)

Below: Fort Benning, 1st Division Road, July 23, 1941. The Army was proud of its new materiel and regularly organized presentations for the American public. Here, from left: a Ford GP Jeep, a Dodge ½-ton command reconnaissance truck, a Dodge ½-ton weapons carrier truck, a Chevrolet 1½-ton YP-G-4112 YJ cargo truck, a GMC 2½-ton CCKWX-353 cargo truck, and a Diamond T 4-ton Model 967 truck. (U.S. Army SC-123995)

Right: After the Engineers, the Field Artillery was the biggest user of the new vehicles in the 4-ton, 6x6 category. Their size and performance were well suited to towing the 155-mm artillery pieces. (U.S. Army Signal Corps)

Below: August 22, 1941, Brooklyn Army Base. Mack and Diamond T967 vehicles are ready to be loaded for overseas service. As they have been given no specific protection, they will do the crossing in the bottom of the hold. (U.S. Army SC-126015)

The Cab

Consisting of an assembly of body panels made rigid by a wooden structure, the cab and its interior fittings were directly derived from civilian productions of the period.

Designed for a crew of three, it had a rubber-covered floor, anti-skid pedal pads and canvas seats. The dashboard had five gauges with incorporated lighting: a rev counter, an air pressure gauge, a viscosity indicator, and a dial showing temperature, oil pressure, and electrical charge. Apart from the side gills at the crew's feet, ventilation was through a panel placed horizontally on the body at the front of the

Below: Engineer pontoon units needed a vehicle in this category because their bridging equipment was long and cumbersome, so they started looking for a suitably adequate vehicle. They had to wait a while before the Diamond T 970 appeared: it was brought out especially for them. This 967 is towing a trailer with an extendable shaft, carrying elements of the Model 1935 footbridge. (Goodyear Co.)

cab and by a small cap fitted with a ventilator on the roof. Unlike many military vehicles of the period, the dashboard did not have a closed glovebox, there being an open compartment set in the upper part.

The general shape of the cab was maintained in subsequent productions, which was not the case with the protective grille.

Right: Preceded by a GMC CCKWX-353, two Diamond T 967s lead a column of heavy Mack NJU-1s of the 87th Heavy Ponton Battalion, Fort Benning, May 1941. (U.S. Army SC-119901)

Below: Fort Benning, 1st Division Road, July 23, 1941, from right: a Ford GP Jeep, a Dodge ½-ton command reconnaissance vehicle, a Dodge ½-ton weapons carrier, a Chevrolet 1½-ton cargo YP-G-4112-YJ truck, a GMC 2½-ton, cargo CCKWX-353 truck, and a Diamond T 4-ton Model 967 truck. (U.S. Army SC-123993)

Right: The cargo technical body which was fitted on the Diamond T 967 remained similar to those on the subsequent series of Model 968s, until the arrival of the all-wood version.

1) Rear fender shield
2) Tailgate step
3) Pintle hook
4) Fender shield steps
5) Rear fender shield
6) Red reflector
7) Tailgate
8) Tailgate chain
9) Seat support leg
10) Seat hinge support
11) Seat board
12) Lazyback board
13) Safety strap
14, 15, 16) Bow, bow top section, bow corners
17) Curtain strap
18) Bow upright
19) Rope hook
20) Fender brace
21) Front fender
22) Red reflector
(Extract from TM10-1605)

On the Model 967, this was a one-piece wrought-iron part which covered the radiator and the headlamps, which were surmounted by small marker lights with bluish lenses. Two large running boards surmounted by large structures gave easy access to the cab; on the left was the gasoline tank and on the right the batteries and wheel chains.

Left: Fort Benning, February 4, 1941, major autumn maneuvers and showing the gap between a Diamond T 967 C cargo truck and a Bantam Jeep, both from C Company, 4th Engineer Battalion, 4th Division. (International News photo ref. 5928408)

Below: August 22, 1941, the 102nd Engineer Ponton Battalion tests the pontoon it has just laid across the Missouri River. It had to enable 19,000 men of the 33rd Infantry Division and their cartage to cross during Second U.S. Army maneuvers. The truck is a Diamond T 967 towing an 8-ton flatbed trailer loaded with a Type D6 or D7 bulldozer. (ACME ref. 617043)

Three shots of the same truck registered as USA-W-418043, a Diamond T 967 from contract no. W-398-QM-8270 dated 1940. It was the 775th vehicle of this type to come off the production lines in February 1941. Two months later, this type was replaced by Models 968 and 970. Each driver and each vehicle spent many hours on training courses to ensure a solid working relationship. (Private Collection)

With a Diamond T 967 as a backdrop, GIs have set up a field workshop specializing in repairing tires. The front of the cargo body shows an American specialty where reflectors were concerned on the trucks: red at the rear and on the sides, and orange at the front. Thus, in the light of the headlamps, a driver would know if what was in front of him was the rear or the front of the obstacle to be avoided and the direction it was facing. (U.S. Army C-269; ACME ref. 617043)

The Body

Produced by Gar Wood Industry, the design was traditional; the base was made entirely of steel with the sides reinforced by a lower and an upper metal strut and five crosspieces also used for positioning the legs of its side rails; on the rear was a large tailgate mounted on a hinged axis providing easy access.

On the sides, two removable wooden rails, made up of six longitudinal slats increased the height of the load area. When the vehicle was in the troop transport configuration, four of these slats were folded down to form benches. The squat shape of the vehicle left no space for the spare wheels other than in the cargo body. On the part near the cabin were two supports which meant the benches were shorter than the side rails, with no frontal rail. As well as their function as spare wheels, these could also be fitted to the front axle wheels in order to provide more traction in soft terrain. Under the cargo part, four vertical mudguards ensured there was a minimum of protection from projectiles that the twinned forward wheels might throw up, those at the rear having three metal rungs and road signal reflectors.

3 The Second Generation

Models 968, 969, & 970

These vehicles were simply the logical development of the Model 967 truck into more accomplished, more solid vehicles with better performance. There were now three designated models in the same category: 968, 969, and 970.

Like all military vehicles, the Diamond T 4x4, 4-ton truck changed and evolved. Although its silhouette remained more or less the same, it was now different because the radiator and headlamp protective grille had been removed and replaced by another that was incorporated into the radiator block with two small protective grilles on the wheel arches, just in front of the lenses. This new grille meant a new casing for the radiator's 11 parts and the radiator cap which, now repositioned instead of being perfectly horizontal, was tilted slightly foward.

This change was caused by the upper water container increasing in size, taking up the extra width created by the new grille.

Apart from this change in the front, the rest of the bodywork, like the cab and the dashboard, remained the same.

The truck chassis' overall layout did not change; the spring leaves were now made of chrome-vanadium steel, and the Houde hydraulic shock absorbers were now BBH models. There was no change in the winch/PTO and accessories. Production started in March 1941 and the following series in the following November.

Below: Side view of the truck at bottom. The overall outline is now defined and the range will evolve from this base. (U.S. Army Signal Corps)

Below: A typical example of a Diamond T 968 from the earliest series, with its registration no. USA-W-457705 taken from the first order, W-398-QM-8926, for 736 vehicles. The new headlamp and radiator protection is in striking contrast to the Diamond T 967's enormous grille.

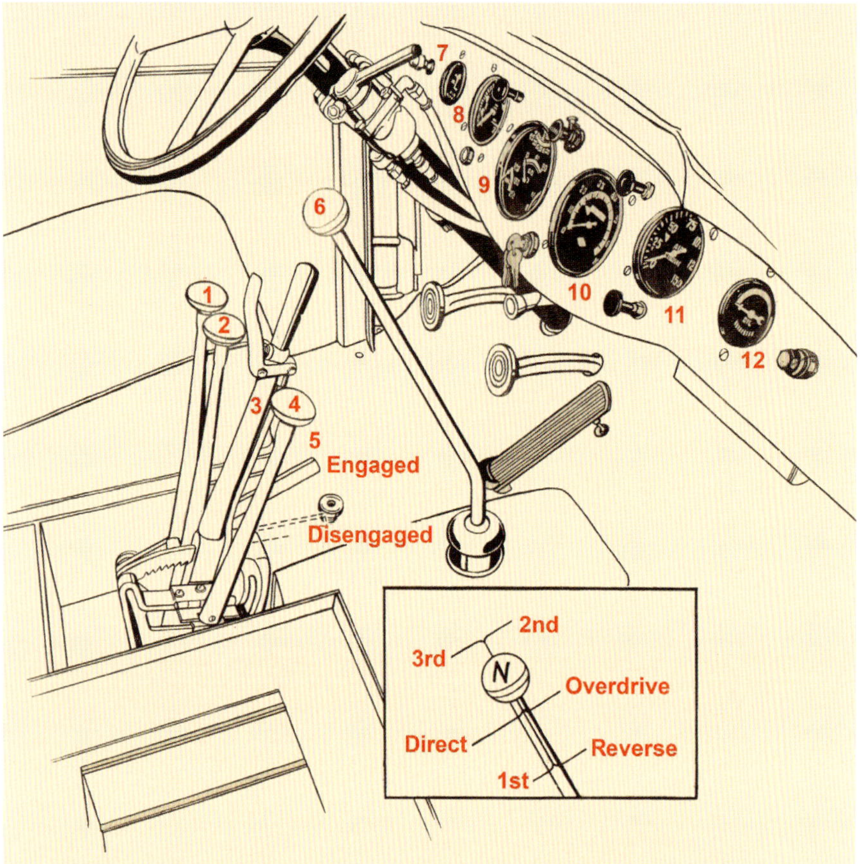

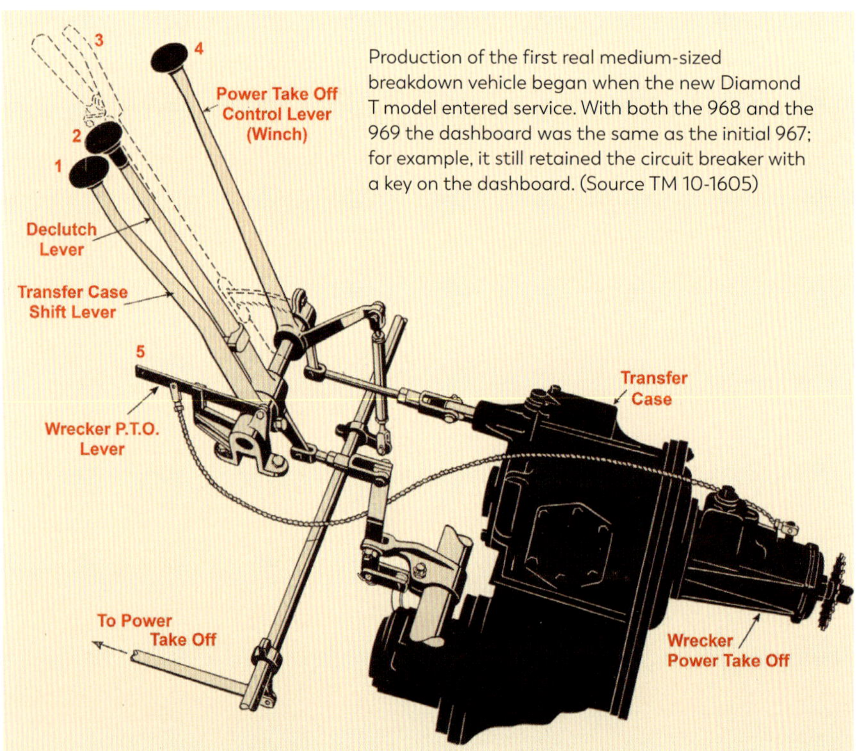

Production of the first real medium-sized breakdown vehicle began when the new Diamond T model entered service. With both the 968 and the 969 the dashboard was the same as the initial 967; for example, it still retained the circuit breaker with a key on the dashboard. (Source TM 10-1605)

The Mechanics

It was the mechanical side that changed the most. Still using 9.00x20 10-ply tires, the second-generation Diamond T was built on three Timken-Detroit Axle Company differentials, of the double reduction type with the reference numbers SFD-154-W for the rear pair and F-2090-TW-73 for the front one. The vehicle was powered by a Hercules Model RXC gasoline engine, which consisted of a single block with six cylinders surmounted by a two-piece cylinder head with side valves. The engine was 8,670.31 cc (529 cubic inches) rated at 131.5 bhp at 2,300 rpm. All this was cooled by a radiator with 11 tubes with winglets and a water pump located on the left-hand side of the engine block. On the front was a new six-blade, 22-inch-diameter ventilator fan to cool the 48 quarts (45.4 liters) in the cooling circuit.

Power was taken to the transmission through a W. C. Lipe Model Z42-S single dry disc clutch, and a Clark Model 326-VO-18 gearbox with five forward and one reverse gears, and a two-speed Wisconsin Model T763 transfer box that was also used to engage the front differential and access six-wheel drive. Thus, with a Zenith Model IN167S carburetor, an AC Model D pump, and a 40-gallon fuel tank, the Diamond T 968, 969, and 970 trucks could cover distances of between 155 and 200 miles.

(Cont'd on page 27)

Above and left: The arrival of the 969 wrecker meant that a PTO was taken off the transfer box and new levers installed inside the cabin.

1) Transfer box lever
2) Declutch lever (front differential)
3) Hand brake
4) Winch lever
5) PTO lever
6) Gear lever
7) Battery level
8) Rev counter
9) Gauges for temperature, amperage, oil pressure, and fuel level.
10) Speedometer
11) Air pressure
12) Viscometer

(Extract from TM 10-1605)

Holabird Quartermaster Depot, Baltimore, December 10, 1941. This is a typical example of a Diamond T 696 wrecker truck from the earliest series with its registration USA-W-003178, taken from the first order W-398-QM-8926 for 507 examples. (U.S. Army SC-127235)

Below: Getting rid of the big protective radiator grille at the front meant that the blackout lamps could not be positioned on the top of the headlamps as on the 967 series. The two elements were now separated, both being positioned on the wing, which meant changing all the electrical connections and cables. (Source TM 10-1603/1605)

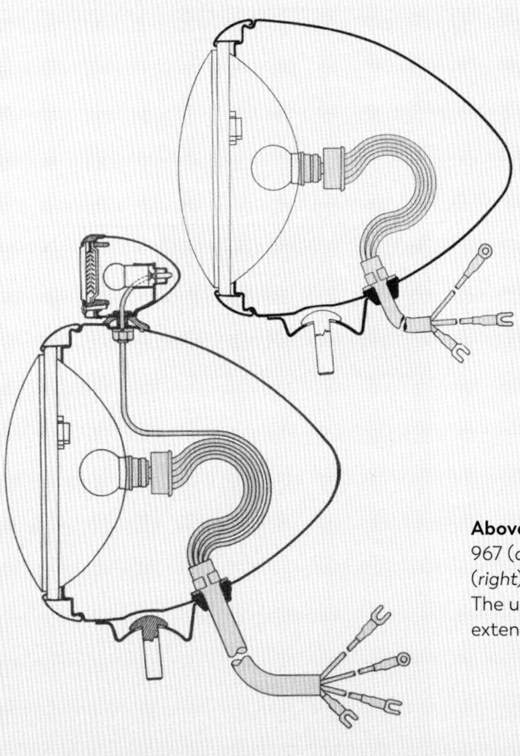

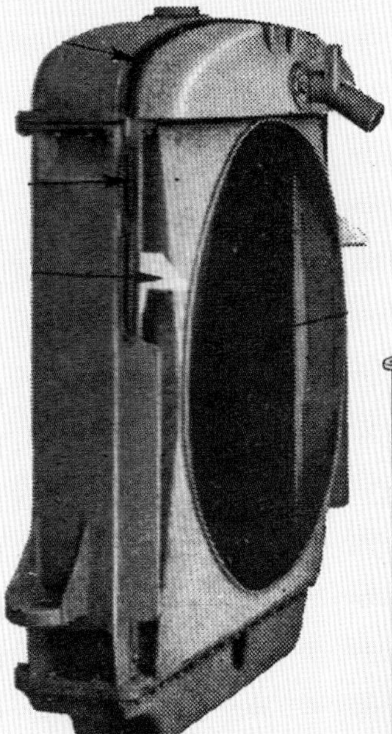

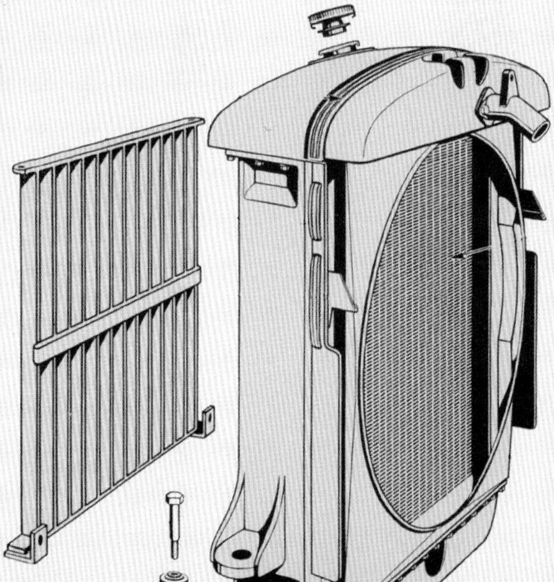

Above and right: Comparing the radiator of the 967 (*above*) with that of the 968, 969, and 970 (*right*), to now incorporate the protective grille. The upper water tank has changed shape and is extended toward the front.

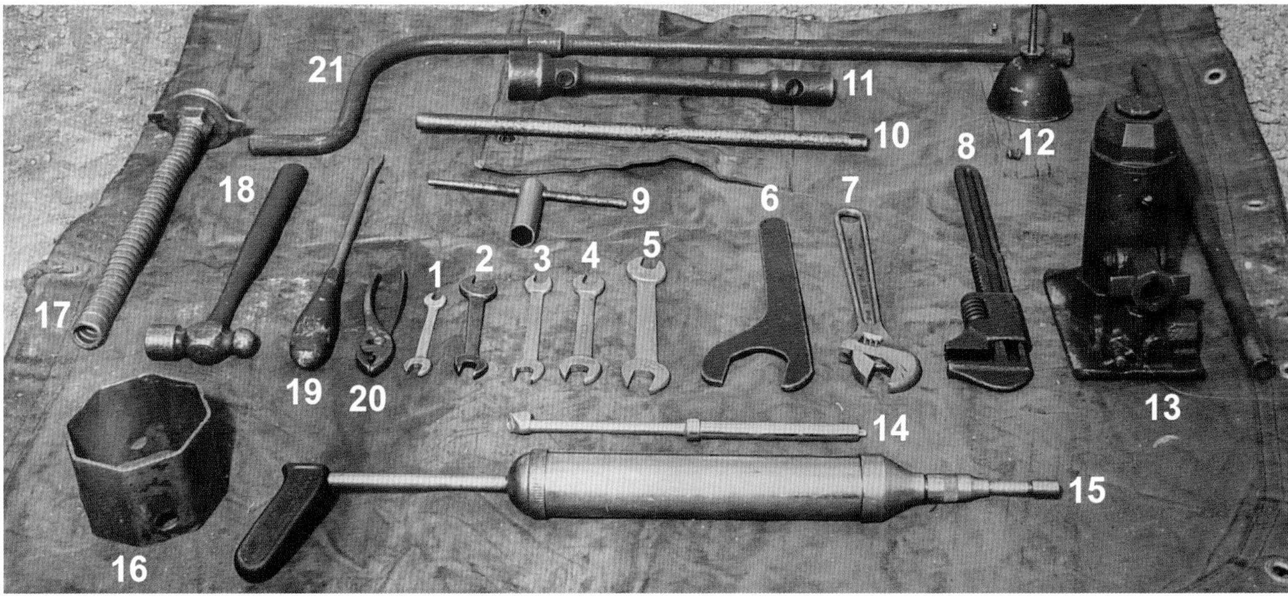

Above: Set out on a truck tarpaulin, the tools which equipped the first deliveries are ready for inspection:

1) 3/8" x 7/16" open-end spanner,
2) 1/2" x 19/32" open-end spanner
3 9/16" x 11/16" open-end spanner
4) 5/8" x 25/32" open-end spanner
5) 3/4" x 7/8" open-end spanner
6 13/16" open-end spanner
7) Adjustable spanner
8) Adjustable wrench
9) Plug spanner
10) Wheel spanner bar
11) Wheel spanner
12) Oil can
13) Jack
14) Tire pressure gauge
15) Grease pump
16) Hub spanner
17) Jerrycan hose
18) Hammer
19) Screwdriver
20) Flat pliers
21) Wheel brace

This selection evolved with time and was greatly enlarged. (U.S. Army SC-146517)

FEATURES OF THE FIRST SERIES COMPARED WITH THE REST OF THE PRODUCTION

Element	First series: 967 Model	Second series: models w/out A or B suffix (968, 969, 970)	Details
Front differential	Timken F-2090-TW-74	Timken F-2090-TW-73	Difference is with bearings, the BB5214 Model becoming the Type 1214
Rear differential	Timken SED-153-TW	Timken SFD-154-W	Difference is with the bearings, 1828E5 Model becoming the Type 1214
Front leaf spring	2 x chrome-vanadium 10 x chrome-manganese	12 x chrome-vanadium	
Shock absorber	Houde BBGH	Houde BBH	
Rear leaf spring	9 x silicon-manganese	9 x chrome-vanadium	
Engine	Hercules RXB 501 cu.in 122 bhp at 2,300 rpm	Hercules RXC 529 cu.in 131.5 bhp at 2,300 rpm	Engine sump oil reduced from 10 to 16 quarts
Clutch	Borg & Beck 14 Q,15 in	W. C. Lipe Z42-S,15 in	
Gearbox	Clark 326-VO-18	Clark 326-VO-18	12-quart oil capacity (11.35 l)
Transfer	Wisconsin T7 M3	Wisconsin T76	Ratio change in low range, 3-quart oil capacity (2.84 l)
Winch PTO	Gar Wood 74 Y 6000	Gar Wood 74 Y 6000	3-quart oil capacity (2.84 l)
Carburetor	Zenith IN167SJ	Zenith IN167SJ	
Fuel pump	AC 'D' series	AC 'D' series	
Fuel filter	Zenith Laminated	Zenith Laminated	
Generator	Autolite GEW-4802	Autolite GEW-4802	
Starter	Autolite ML-4209	Autolite ML-4209	
Distributor	Autolite IGC-4286	Autolite IGC-4701	
Regulator	Autolite VRY-4201A	Autolite VRY-4201A	
Steering box	Ross T-71	Ross T-71	
Winch	Gar Wood 3U-615	Gar Wood 3U-615	
Battery	Autolite T-2-15,118A/hr	Exide XH-194.152A/hr	In both cases, the installation is positive earthed
Wheel rims	Budd 44460	Budd 44460	
Fuel tank	40 gallons	40 gallons	

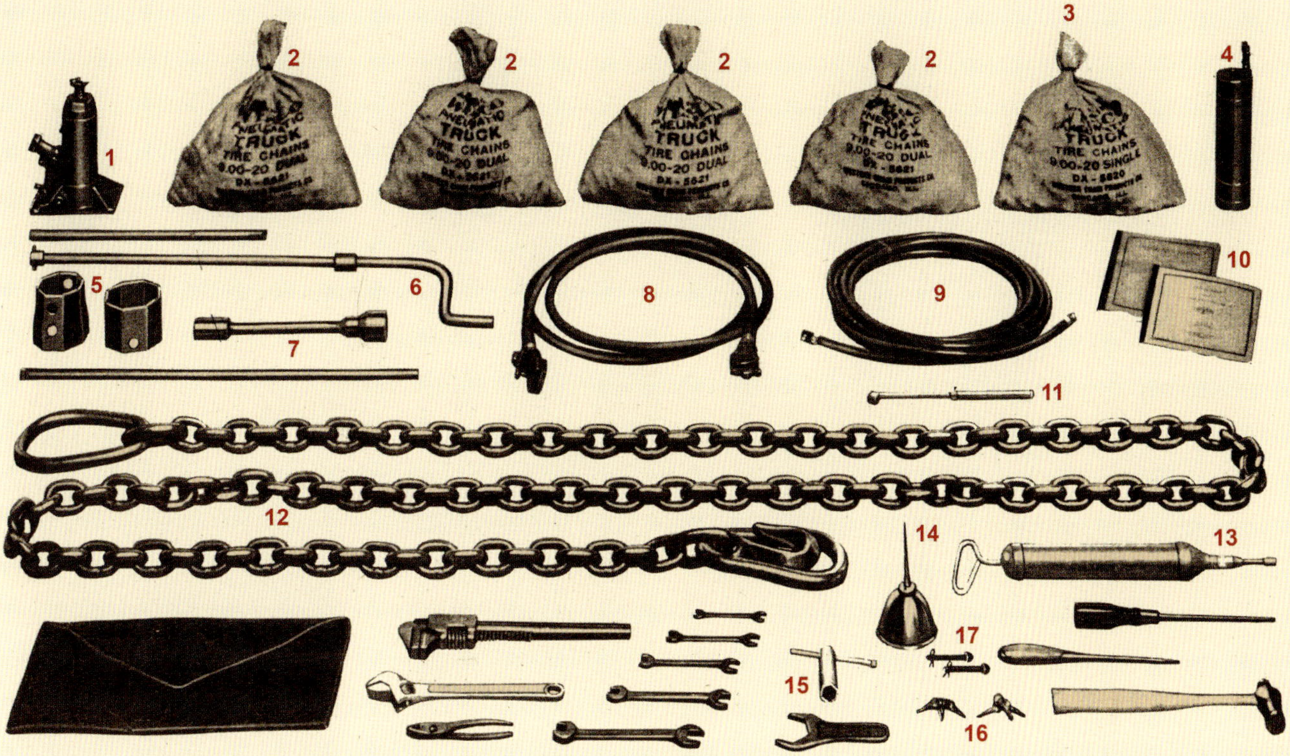

The onboard toolkit assortment evolved considerably, enabling crews to become more autonomous. It now consisted of:

1) Jack
2) Set of snow chains for the twinned wheels
3) Set of snow chains for the single wheels
4) Cabin fire extinguisher
5) Hub spanner for front and rear wheels
6) Wheel brace
7) Wheel extension
8) Joining hose for the pneumatic trailer brake joint
9) Hose for inflating the tires
10) Technical manual and spare parts catalog
11) Tire pressure gauge
12) Towing chain
13) Grease pump
14) Oil can
15) Hand tools
16) Ignition key and tachymeter key
17) Winch pin

(Source TM 10-1533)

(Cont'd from Page 24)

This gave a consumption rate of between 3.85 and 5 mpg, depending on the terrain covered and the driving conditions.

As for the electrical installation, this worked on two 6-volt batteries giving 152 amps/hour.

The light casings were also changed, the little marker lights with bluish lenses being replaced by blackout fender lights which remained for the rest of the production and were thereafter located on the wings.

Sgt Herzog from the 481st Light Ponton Company poses with his 970. The side rails were fragile and often modified in the field which enabled heavier loads to be carried beyond those specified. (Private Collection)

A test being carried out fully loaded with 11.00x20 tires. Mobility remained one of the priorities and a major worry for the Ordnance Department which continually tried to improve vehicle capabilities in extreme conditions. (Private Collection)

The spare parts box appeared in 1944 containing a strict minimum of spare parts, stored away in the vehicle cab:

A) Spare parts box
B) Blackout tail lamp unit
C) Stop/rear light bulb
D) Stop/rear light blackout bulb
E) Two fanbelts
F) A box of crimping pins
G) Iron baling wire
H) Spark plug
I) Blackout marker lamp bulb
J) A set of tire valves
K) A set of valve caps
L) A roll of wire for ligatures
M) Four safety pins for the winch
(Source TM 9-811)

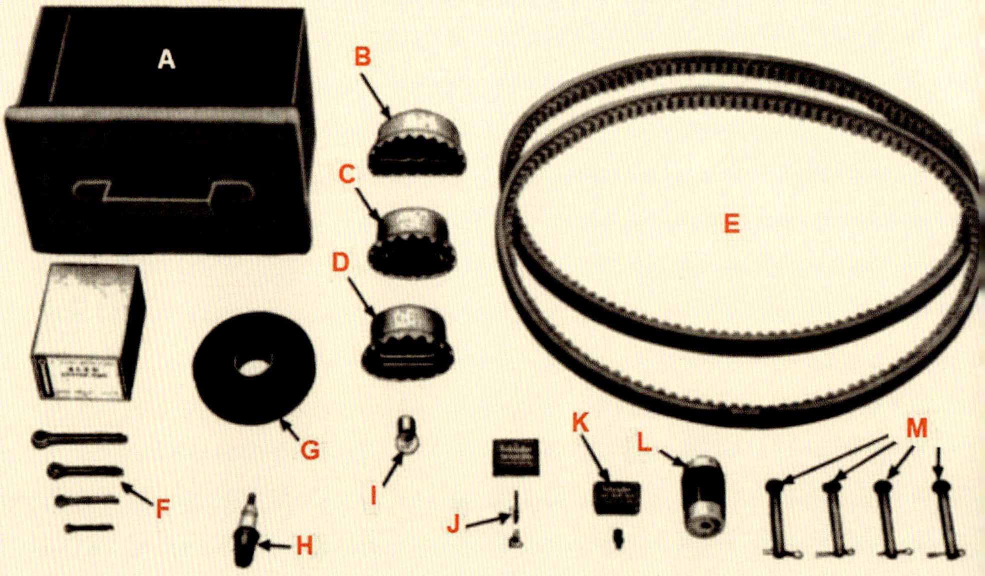

4 The Third Generation

Models 968A, 969A, & 970A/968B, 969B, & 970B

With this new production, the Diamond Ts came of age; it was a period of large contracts and mass production. All the models had a suffix with their designation, either an A or a B, to differentiate from previous series.

In September 1941, production of the first vehicles designated 968A, 969A, and 970A began. It was not until February 1943 that the Model 972 dump truck appeared which, strangely enough, was never given an A suffix but had all the particularities of the other three. (One cannot really speak of new vehicles per se but rather of developments, with all that that implied in modifications and variants.)

The A-suffixed Vehicles

The general shape, the chassis, and the mechanics remained absolutely unchanged with the start of this new production, the main differences being military.

The appearance of the blackout drive lamps on the front left wing partly modified the electrical circuit meaning new electrical tresses. The positioning of the lamp between the hood flank and the headlamp meant that a new wrought-iron grille was required with an extra section on the side that was to be seen only on the 972s and the A suffixes. The dashboard was changed; its civilian gauges disappeared and were replaced entirely by standardized military models, their number increasing from six to nine. The backlighting was removed and replaced by three small overhanging spotlights. All these changes meant new bodywork and new casting stamps had to be made.

Above: Lashio, Burma, April 10, 1945. As well as add-ons in the field like the front fenders and the search lamps on the cabin, this Diamond T 969A has all the signs of being from the final development. The protective grille on the left headlamp includes the blackout drive lamp, the Diamond T logo has disappeared from the vehicle nose, and the doors have handles on the reinforcement casing. (U.S. Army SC-317787)

Right: The arrival of the tarpaulin-covered cab was the last major development of the Diamond T chassis outline. The cab body changed without the dashboard changing. (Private Collection)

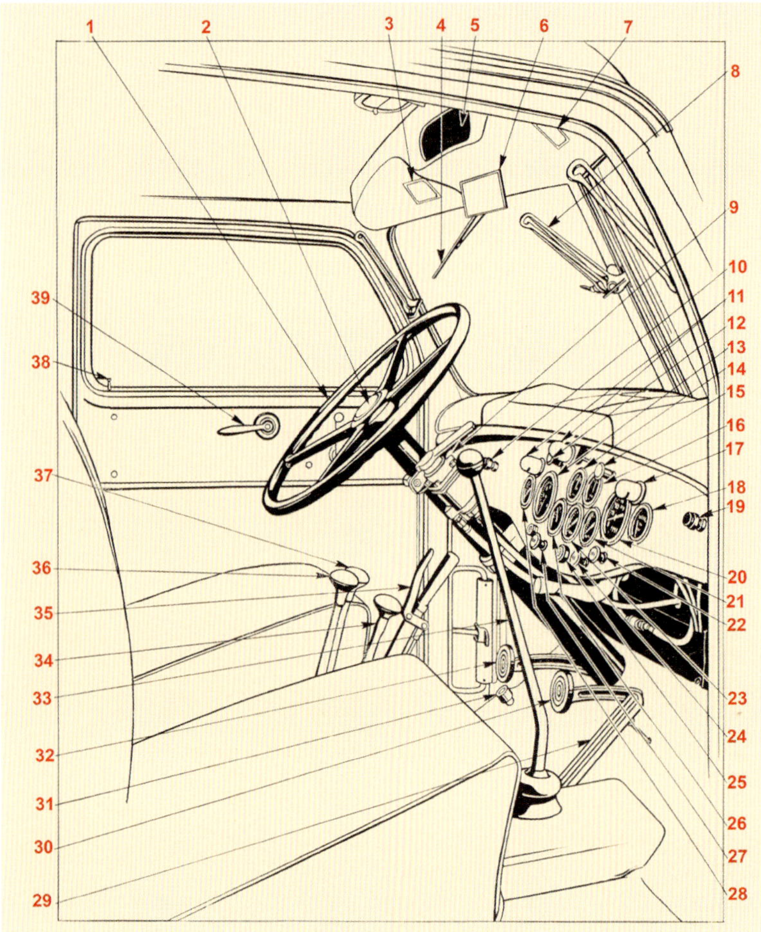

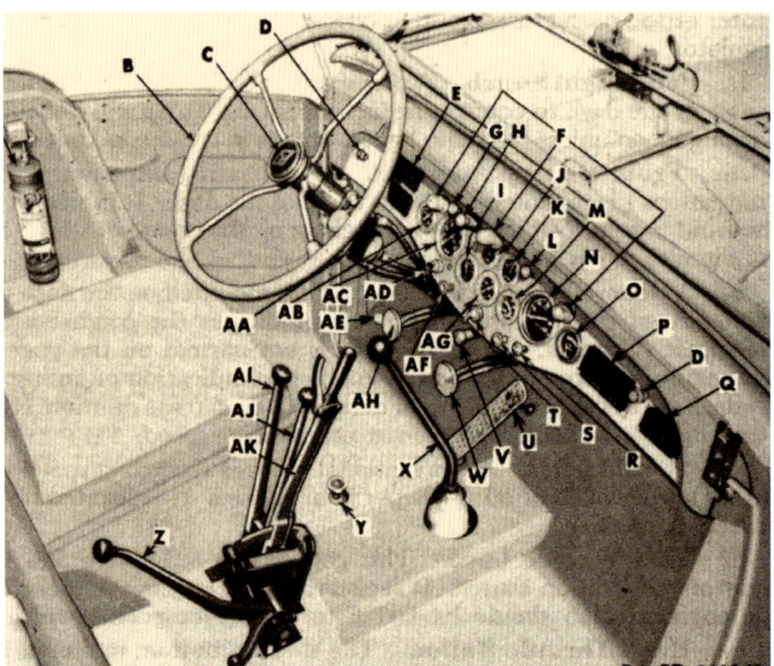

Left: The inside of the covered cab of the A suffixes:

1) Steering wheel
2) Horn button
3) Instruction plate
4) Windshield wiper
5) Glove compartment
6) Rear view mirror
7) Instruction plate
8) Windshield sector arm
9) Hand air brake control
10) Windshield wiper control
11) Dashboard lights
12) Main light switch
13) Tachometer
14) Ammeter
15) Dashboard panel light switch
16) Ammeter
17) Dashboard lights
18) Viscometer
19) Windshield wiper control
20) Speedometer
21) Temperature gauge
22) Hand throttle button
23) Oil pressure gauge
24) Choke button
25) Ignition switch
26) Fuel gauge
27) Advance/retard control
28) Air pressure gauge
29) Accelerator pedal
30) Brake pedal
31) Headlight switch
32) Clutch pedal,
33) Transmission lever
34) Power takeoff shift lever (winch)
35) Hand brake lever
36) Declutching lever
37) Transfer case shift lever
38) Safety lock
39) Handle

(Source TM 10-1607)

Strangely enough, various other minor modifications soon appeared. The builder's logo disappeared from the radiator, as it did with all the other firms. The official line was to remove all civilian markings and give military vehicles more of a universal character.

Below: 852nd Ordnance Battalion at Camp Claiborne in Louisiana, December 1, 1942. (U.S. Army SC-166324)

Left: The layout of the open cabin was roughly unchanged; note that the small instruction plates are no longer on the cabin fronton but are now on the dashboard. The steering wheel has become easier to make with its simpler spokes. (Source TM9-811)

The tool and battery box located on the right-hand running board definitively became an impressed version with cross-like folds to make its structure more rigid. The increase in the diameter of the tank filler also meant that the metal structure for the hole had to be modified.

Even stranger and for no apparent reason, new doors appeared. This modification was noticeable by the handle which was positioned higher up and was now straight instead of curved. The stiffening of the door's horizontal casing was repositioned, meaning that internal modifications were made to the mechanism and to the position of the latch.

In May 1943, the open cab was standardized and once and for all replaced the all-metal cab. Actually, this new cab was the result of an in-depth study carried out on low-silhouette vehicles: from among all the prototypes tested, only one vehicle from Dodge and one from Ford were mass-produced, the main lesson learned from this study being that the imposing all-metal cabs in all types of military cartage were fragile, cumbersome, and voluminous. These could simply be replaced by newer models with foldable upper parts and tarpaulin roofs, thereby reducing the vehicle's volume. This particularity was appreciated when vehicles had to pack into confined holds for transport overseas. Unlike the all-metal cabs whose structure was not included in the spare parts inventory, all the elements of this new type were readily available on parts lists.

Chronologically, this new Diamond T configuration appeared from chassis no. 968A-4390, 969A-3029, and 970A-0495 onward.

From November 1941 to August 1945 things were generally fluid with many changes made during the production cycle: the camshaft was modified, there were changes to the oil filter and the engine filler, the ventilator for the lower part of the engine was improved, and new types of water pump, air filter, and distributor replaced the initial models. Each of these changes can be found by going through the voluminous documentation, SNL G-509.

Above: In the Lekha-Pani region of India, the 382nd Engineer Construction Battalion takes part in reconstructing a section of railway. While the GMC CCKW-353 pours ballast into a wagon, the 968A pushes it. The latter is a later version with a tarpaulin-covered cabin and a wooden cargo body. The gas tank filler opening is the wide version and tilted slightly to make filling easier. The tank's protective plate is fitted with eight fastening points enabling, for example, the pioneers' toolbox to be attached to it. (U.S. Army SC-2577452)

1945, in the Ehrbach region, Bade-Wurtemberg, near the Danube. These GIs from the 481st Engineer Light Ponton Company pose proudly in front of their Diamond T 968A trucks. Delivered in 1942, this example has crossed half the continent to end its travels in a peaceful region. (968A, USA-458892, contract W-398-QM-9568.) (Private Collection)

The B-suffixed Vehicles

There were only two designations in this category, the 968B and the 969B, used for those vehicles especially destined for Canada and, in far fewer numbers, to Great Britain. These were not vehicles without a suffix or A variants, but rather a sort of hybrid of the two with particular specifications requested by Canada and Great Britain. As the electrical installation comprised no blackout lamps and only one main headlamp, the two protective grilles were not fitted. These B variants were painted in what was called COD (Canadian Olive Drab), which differed from the American Army's OD.

Puzzling

Despite extreme precision in all administrative documents concerning the technical side of the 4-ton, 6x6 vehicles, there remain a certain number of puzzles for which there is no explanation to this day.

The most surprising conundrum concerns fuel capacity, either 40 or 60 gallons; the idea of the 60-gallon tank only appeared in the generalized versions of the Technical Manual-2800. Even more surprising, the TM-9811 dated January 25, 1944, on page 161, mentions a 40-gallon fuel capacity, whereas on page 168, it gives the capacity as 60 gallons.

It is therefore impossible to determine when this modification was made. Whatever transpired, with this increased quantity, vehicle performances changed. The range, originally between 155 and 200 miles, increased with the extra fuel to between 230 and 280 miles, depending on the type of terrain and the driving conditions.

5 Cargo Trucks

Models 968 & 968A

A total of 1,380 Diamond T Model 968s and 7,321 Model 968As were supplied and taken on charge under the designation Cargo Truck. These were standard vehicles with a short wheelbase, in current use, and widely distributed among the units.

These 4-ton, 6x6 trucks were not used for any particular specialty apart from the fact that they belonged to a category in which power made them excellent workers where strength was required. The body could just as easily be used for transporting troops as it could for equipment. Their shape and mechanics evolved along with the whole range just like the other models. All 968s were fitted with an all-metal cabin and six dials, and all 968As had a dashboard with nine dials. During production the 968As were fitted with a tarpaulin-covered cabin, this change coming into effect with chassis no. 968A-4390.

It is commonly accepted that 8,653 Diamond T 968As were ordered; this is verifiable on the lists of orders addressed to the manufacturer, but only 7,321 examples were taken on charge up to August 1945 according to the monthly production inventory. There are only two possible causes for this difference of 1,332 units. Either supplies were continued after the accounts/deductions were established for auditing the current orders, or the production lines were ordered to halt abruptly. Also counted in the Lend-Lease delivery statistics were 1,556 Diamond T 4-ton, 6x6 cargo trucks, which were supplied to the Allied nations:

654th Engineer Topographic Battalion, Marburg, Germany, 1945. An all-metal cab and wooden cargo body for this Diamond T cargo truck, with the pretty name of *Leona*. As an infrequent modification, a traverse was fitted between the bumper and the mudguard. As the gap between them was relatively wide, this piece of metal prevented branches or small trees from jamming the truck. (Model 968A, USA-444930, contract no. W-398-QM-W-662.) (Private Collection)

Oppposite: November 27, 1941, during maneuvers in Pennsylvania, the 103rd Engineer Construction Battalion has just thrown a makeshift crossing over a small watercourse. The decisive test was to get a GMC CCKWX-353 across it. Engineer units were widely supplied with these Diamond T trucks for transporting their heavy, cumbersome equipment. (968, USA-W-458831, contract no. W-398QM-9568.) (ACME ref. 628992)

753 to Great Britain, 265 to France, 67 to China, 38 to Brazil, three to Latin American countries, 29 to the USSR, and 400 to Canada.

The Cargo Body

This was unquestionably the vehicle's cornerstone, designed so that there were no restrictions as to its use where transport was concerned: it consisted of an all-metal platform with three vertical sides and a rear tailgate. On the front side were two mounts for the spare wheels placed on the inside.

Given the position of the spare wheels, the benches were shorter than the side rails themselves and there was no front rail on the 968/968As.

Inactive signaling comprised six reflectors, one on each rear mudguard and one on the rear of each side of the body; these four reflectors were red. On the front of the cargo part and clearly visible were two others, orange, on either side of the cab.

Above: The rear side of an early-production metal body; the lamps were inset in relation to the body and the rear reflectors were fitted to the mudguards, just between the two upper echelons. (968, USA-W-457490, contract no. W-398-QM-8926.) (Private Collection)

Below: Toward the end of 1942, the Army initiated a comprehensive study of how tires behaved in various conditions; the Diamond Ts took part, extensively testing different types of tires, like here with 11.00x20s in sandy terrain. (968A, USA-W-486568, contract no. W-398-QM-10998.) (US Army Signal Corps)

Right: It was trugged trial work for the standard vehicles which endured thousands of miles over difficult, rocky terrain in order to try and define what was needed to keep the vehicle fleet operational. (968A, USA-W-461615, contract no. W-398-QM-10140.)

Built by Edward G. Budd Manufacturing Company, these metal bodies were slightly modified several times with the appearance of the 968As, the most obvious being the rear light supports. When production started, these were some distance from the vehicle's rear face and hidden under the platform; then for ease of access, the covers of the lenses were positioned practically flush with the rear face and the mounts shortened, and the two reflectors located on the mudguards were placed on the tailgate.

From April 1943, the 968As were fitted with wooden cargo bodies to save on steel. These structures were made by various carpentry workshops, including furniture and piano makers, enabling 1,102.31 lb of steel to be saved per unit.

(Cont'd on page 41)

Left: January 13, 1942, at Holabird Quartermaster Depot, Baltimore. This brand-new Diamond T is on the test track and is descending a 60% slope. For each evolution on whichever vehicle, the Army carried out regular tests to ensure supplies were up to standard. (968A, USA-W-482073, contract no. W-398-QM-10140.)

Above: It took several stages of development before a particular place was found for the pioneers' tool rack. In the meantime, it was placed in a variety of positions, like the side of the cargo body, however, the tarpaulin would would chafe against it. (968, USA-W-457769, contract no. W-398-QM-8926.)

Below: Clearly visible is the lack of a front rail due to the spare tires and the bench being shorter than the side rail. The cab door is from the second production series, with the handle situated on the stiffening rib. (968A, USA-W-4111361, contract no. W-398-QM-11509.) (Private Collection)

DIAMOND T MODEL 968 CARGO TRUCK PRODUCTION	
Chassis numbers 970-0001 to 970-1234 = 1,234 vehicles, all with a metal cab, from contract no. W-398-QM-8926, all taken on charge in 1941.	(457477 to 458210) + (458212 to 458217) + (458219 to 458226) + (458228 to 458231) + (458243 to 458247) + (458252 to 458255) + (458259 to 458267) + (458270 to 458273) + (458275 to 458278) + (458280 to 458282) + (458284 to 458288) + (458290 to 458293) + (458295 to 458297) + (458302 to 458305) + (458307 to 458310) + (458312 to 458315) + (458323 to 458325) + (458330 to 458333) + (458338 to 458347) + (458349 to 458353) + (458355 to 458376) + (458378 to 458396) + (458399 to 458435) + (458437 to 458466) + (458468 to 458470) + (458527 to 458796) + 458234, 458240, 458249, 458250, 458257, 458299, 458300, 458317, 458318, 458328, 458335, 458336, 458320, 458472, 458475, 458480, 458481, 458491, 458494, 458509, 458518, 458801, 458803, 458828, 458851, 458853.
Chassis numbers 970-1235 to 970-1380 = 146 vehicles, all with a metal cab, from contract no. W-398-QM-9568, all taken on charge in 1941.	(458821 to 458826) + (458829 to 458835) + (458854 to 458856) + (458858 to 458860) + (458862 to 458864) + (458866 to 458872) + (458874 to 458878) + (458880 to 458886) + (458888 to 458950) + (458953 to 458957) + (458959 to 458966) + (458968 to 458973) + (458977 to 458982) + 458819, 458837, 458839, 458841, 458846, 458848, 458850, 458852, 458975, 458984, 458986, 458988, 458989, 458991, 458994, 458999, 459000.
Or a total of 1,380 Model 968 cargo trucks, all with all-metal cab.	

The power of the Diamond T 968 is highlighted here. On the radiator protective grille are the early unit markings of the 150th Field Artillery Battalion. The vehicle has all the features from the first generation. (U.S. Army Signal Corps)

Left: A Diamond T 968A being put through its paces over rugged terrain. (U.S. Army Signal Corps)

Below: Company A, 320th Engineer Combat Battalion of the 9th Infantry Division, Fort Sam Houston, Texas, March 16, 1943. A working configuration towing an 8-ton trailer carrying a small D4. (968A, USA-W-4110884, contract no. W-398-QM-11509.) (U.S. Army SC-171870)

Right: Clearing away rubble blocking the roads was also one of the Engineers' duties. It is June 23, 1944 on rue Jeanne d'Arc in Montebourg, on the Cotentin Peninsula and the town has just been liberated. Situated between Sainte-Mère Église and Cherbourg, a few miles from Utah Beach, this was a vital area for resupplying the American Army. (U.S. Army Signal Corps)

Middle: Somewhere in England, April 8, 1944, in one of the many ordnance repair depots where workshops are fully occupied due to intensive ongoing maneuvers. In the middle are Dodges, Whites, Jeeps, GMCs, and two Diamond Ts; on the right is the rear of a 972 dump truck and on the left a cargo truck of the 356th Engineer Battalion. (968A, USA-4553943, contract no. W-271-ORD-4577.)

Below left: Off-road tires were not an absolute guarantee on muddy, slippery roads. The driver of this Diamond T 968 has just realized this by taking a bend on the Lumley Road, near Reykjavik, Iceland, too quickly. Given the position of the winch cable, it is not the first time that this truck has faced traction issues. (U.S. Army SC-133014)

Below right: The position of the load leaves no doubt why this truck left the road: going too fast around a long bend caused the whole load to slide outward. Vehicles with large cargo holds had no fastening points to ensure that heavy loads were secured, as this driver from the 21st Engineer Battalion has just discovered, November 26, 1941. (U.S. Army SC-133014)

Left: Okinawa, June 7, 1945. Tracked cranes unload supplies from barges at the docks. The goods are loaded directly onto vehicle cargo bodies. Outside these zones set up by the Engineers, communication channels were very slippery which meant that crews had to fit chains to improve mobility. In the background is a rare FWD HAR-1n 4x4 truck. (U.S. Army Signal Corps)

Below left: January 1945, northern Italy, in the foothills of the Alps near Collina, a Diamond T defies the rigors of winter. Belonging to the 175th Engineer Regiment of the Fifth U.S. Army, this vehicle has all its unit markings on one side of the fender. (U.S. Army SC-198866)

Below right: Destination Russia for this Diamond T 968, making a stop on an Iranian road in 1943 in what was known as the Persian Corridor. Each column had its beast of burden such as this, a vehicle capable of towing and winching, to assist the convoy in rough terrain. (U.S. Army Signal Corps)

relatively easy to put together, but the wood could only take so much weight.

Although the bottom was strong enough, the same cannot be said of the sides which were under a great deal of pressure from the force exerted against them and exacerbated by the instability of the benches on the structure.

After January 1945, there were fewer restrictions on steel and wooden bodies were abandoned in favor of reintroducing steel bodies, which was the case with the penultimate order for 969A cargo trucks, contract no. W-271-ORD-11-022-240 with 561 Diamond T 968As. Note that the last buying order (contract no. W-271-ORD-11-022-289) for 2,261 cargo vehicles was cut by 1,274 units and 987 were delivered as 42 bare chassis versions with the remaining 922 converted to Model 972 dump trucks.

Above: Positioning spare wheels in the cargo body was a challenge when transporting loads. Several crews kept only one spare, positioned on the side. (U.S. Army Signal Corps)

Below: Bastogne, Belgium, the 969th Field Artillery Battalion deploys with 155-mm guns, December 29, 1944. The machine gun installed on the left was uncommon. (U.S. Army SC-198295)

Above: July 13, 1944, this Diamond T 968A is being loaded onto a cargo ship. It belongs to the 21st Field Artillery Battalion of the 5th Infantry Division. It will depart its Icelandic port to reach Utah Beach a few days later where it will join the rest of the division that landed on July 9. (U.S. Army SC-191301)

Left: A perfect example of the limitations of the all-wood cargo bodies which quickly became misshapen because of the pressures exerted by the loads. (U.S. Army SC-191301)

Overleaf: Color advertisement in the *Saturday Evening Post*, April 4, 1942.

DIAMOND T TRUCKS

With the colors...for the duration

DIAMOND T will build you even finer Super-Service Trucks than those which serve you today, when Victory brings Peace. Higher mileages with less wear, still more outstanding fuel economy, even greater reliability, safer and swifter road performance—these will recompense you for your contributions to the nation's security.

Diamond T Trucks by many thousands are earning their "service stripes" with our armies today, just as other Diamond T Trucks did in 1917. Their sound engineering, which has served you so well through 30 years of peace-time progress, now serves America just as faithfully.

Your utmost care in the maintenance of your present trucks and the necessary limitation of our output of Diamond T Trucks even for vital commercial service, will find reward in the Victory for which we all must give our every effort.

DIAMOND T MOTOR CAR COMPANY
CHICAGO, ILLINOIS

DIAMOND T
Trucks

6 Wrecker Trucks

Models 969 & 969A

A total of 570 Diamond T Model 969s and 5,913 Model 969As were supplied and taken on charge under the designation Wrecker Truck. These were standard vehicles with a short wheelbase, in contemporary use and widely distributed between units.

The term "wrecker" here takes on its proper meaning since the 969s and the 969As were the first real medium-sized breakdown vehicles which the Army ordered. (Up until then the term applied to vehicles with no lifting capability at all.) These were cargo trucks which used the name and were represented by a registration number starting with a double 0, intended to be fitted with the traditional Lot No. 7 and its lifting gantry, created in 1937. This configuration being distinct in the orders for the GMC ACKWX, CCKWX, and CCKW, the Ward LaFrance Model 106s, the White 950 x 6s, and the Autocar C-7066s, the designation applied therefore also to the more lightweight categories, like the Dodge WC-5, -12, and -14. As the Quartermaster Corps supplied the vehicles, each user equipped them according to his own needs.

Above: The rear was very typical; this is a 968 from early production with a cargo body, the lights of which are not flush with the rear of the body. The large reflectors were added later by the crew. The markings are those of a Medium Maintenance (MM) Ordnance Company, Second U.S. Army. (Private Collection)

Below: There were a multitude of extra "personal" fittings on these breakdown trucks. On this example is a storage basket on the top of the crane gantry, jerrycans on the running boards and on the inside of the rear mudguards. This is a vehicle from the Ninth Air Force, Europe, October 29, 1944. (U.S. Army Air Forces)

Top: A view of the right-hand side showing the position of the fire extinguisher and the shortening of the access panel to the storage space under the cab, and the regulation position for the towing bar with its clevis pin. (Model 969, USA-W-003178, contract no. W-398-QM-8926.) (U.S. Army SC-134742)

Above: The same truck from the other side, with rubberized strips fitted to its rear tires which were supposed to increase traction on soft terrain. (U.S. Army SC-134741)

Right: Diamond Ts participated widely in the Army's tire assessment program in late 1942, testing various types of tires, such as here with 11.00x20s in sandy conditions. (Model 969, USA-W-003370, contract W-398-QM-8926.) (U.S. Army Signal Corps)

With the arrival of the Diamond T wreckers, a whole new policy was set in motion: the medium-sized breakdown vehicles were delivered entirely fitted out, according to the policy of standardization. It was really a mobile workshop that the Army wanted.

As well as a double jib gantry, the 969/969As were also given "lots" of tools, making them independent of the fixed workshops, and so they could carry out breakdown repairs directly in the field. They were equipped with:

- Lot No. 5 Welding Equipment for welding and cutting operations;
- Lot No. 3 Air Equipment, consisting mainly of an air compressor which in the case of the Diamond Ts was either from Wilbiss or Kellog;
- Lot No. 9 Ground Anchor to anchor the vehicle to the ground;
- and part of Lot No. 7 Wrecking with its towbar and its clevis pin. Naturally this equipment was not complete without the various pulleys, chains, and other V-shaped towbars.

The Shape

If one ignores the technical part, the 969/969As were identical to the 968/968As and mounted on the same 151-inch wheelbase but for two exceptions. To operate the crane winches, the transfer box had a PTO on its rear side operated by a lever in the driving cab and, in order to take the big fire extinguisher on the front right-hand running board, the access panel to the under-cabin stowage space was shortened.

The rear part of the vehicle consisted of several elements, an all-steel body fitted with two large

toolboxes, plus a tailgate enabling it to carry loads, and a gantry for its breakdown and maintenance jobs.

The gantry comprised a gearbox linked by shafts to the PTO located at the rear of the transfer box, and two winches with 200 feet of cable working alone or coupled, each serving one of the lifting jibs. There were also two extendable stabilizing jacks and two manual winches to control the angle of the jibs. These were the principal elements making up the Portique Model W-45 HD made by the Ernest Holmes Company. With a nominal power of 5 tons, the Diamond T 969/969A was able to work using the strength of one gantry only, with the advantage over all other types of breakdown vehicles in the Army in that it was able to swing its jibs round through more than 90° in relation to the longitudinal axis of the truck. The vehicle thus had a towing power of 25,000 lb on road and 11,000 lb off road. In the case where the jibs lifted the front of the vehicle being towed, the authorized weight was only 6,000 lb.

The second element of the technical part was the small cargo body. It went through several minor changes with the appearance of the 969As, the most visible being the rear light mountings. At the start of production, these were some distance from the rear face of the vehicle, hidden under the platform; then, for reasons of ease of access, the lens covers were positioned almost flush with the rear side, the mountings having been shortened.

Above: Fort Leonard Wood, January 9, 1942. When the wrecker showed off for the camera, it provided this remarkable shot. In reality, men from the 6th Quartermaster Battalion are trying to get another vehicle out of the garbage dump it has fallen into. Even the front winch is in action, which was still not enough to prevent the truck's nose from bucking. Note the fender extensions to prevent branches and detritus from slipping under the front of the wing. (Model 969, USA-W-003133, contract no. W-398-QM-8926.) (U.S. Army SC-133317)

Below: The 969/969As were allocated two spare wheels, one fixed to the crossbeam and other inside the cargo body. Crews quite often made a mount to save space. (Private Collection)

Evolution

The 969/969As were general-purpose vehicles and were prevalent in almost all units. As they had been comprehensively designed, they only went through a standard development process, like the rest of the 4-ton, 4x4 vehicles from Diamond T; additionally, the height of the gantry meant that an open cab was not an absolute necessity, which had an impact on production.

Top: This version has a facility for erecting a camouflaged tarpaulin. The hoops are stowed against the cab and the body has an extra intermediary reinforcement. (Model 969A, USA-1110204, contract no. W-398-QM-11509).

Middle and bottom: Coming from the War Department Modification Work Order (a circular for modification after delivery) dated August 21, 1944, these two extracts are explicit, showing how the various hoops are positioned and the tarpaulin set up, the main feature being the last upright, doubled and articulated. (Source MWO ORD G-509-W3)

DIAMOND T MODEL 969 WRECKER TRUCK PRODUCTION			
Qtys	Orders	Registration Numbers	Comments
507	W-398-QM-8926	003115 to 003621	All taken on charge in 1941
Or a total of 507 Model 969 wrecker trucks, all with a metal cab.			

A camouflaging program, begun in October 1943, to make the outline of water and fuel tankers less visible by installing hoops and tarpaulins was also applied to the Diamond T wreckers. This consisted of modifying the sides of the rear body to install the hoop fittings, the number of vertical reinforcements increasing from three to four. The conversion was carried out by placing an offset support on the lifting gantry which served as the first hoop and also a storage rack for the others when not in use. With three simple hoops and two others articulated to form the rear of the camouflage system, the kit included special tarpaulins to cover everything.

Since they were the major cartage component, users gave the wreckers much attention and did not hesitate in improving performance by:

- installing a second or even a third fender to use the truck as a pusher
- installing hoists to increase its handling capabilities
- installing a searchlight on the cabin
- recovering GMC CCKW AA defense modules

It was most certainly this last conversion that was the most ingenious: piercing the cab's metal roof, making a manhole and mounting the M-32 ring mount on the structure of the crane gantry. Parts from the M-32 ring mount usually used on the open-cab version were also fitted.

Within the Lend-Lease program and setting aside 606 Model 969Bs, 729 Model 969/969As were supplied to the Allies. As mentioned, Great Britain received 526, France 112, China 73, Brazil 15, and, in a rather anecdotal manner, three were delivered to Latin American countries.

One of these breakdown trucks, 969A-0555, had a rather special history. Bought by the Canadian armed forces for evaluation, it was the only one supplied in this form.

Above: Crest, southern France, August 31, 1944. The 734th Ordnance Battalion recovers a Panzer III. This example of a 969A is in itself a summary of all the modifications: the original fuel tank has been replaced by a bigger one, a ring-mount M-32 machine gun has been fitted to the gantry, a liaison bar between the fender and the mudguards has been inserted, a front towing hook has been fitted, and the door has been personalized. The vehicle also has a special cargo body which can be fitted with hoops. (U.S. Army SC-193814)

Left: In the Belgian sector of the 84th Infantry Division, January 1945, the Diamond T winches handle the lifting of a Jeep with ease. (U.S. Army SC-199078)

Above left: The 969/969As had become indispensable for all heavy mechanical operations, even on assembly lines: Townsville, Australia, with the 179th Ordnance Battalion. (U.S. Army SC-199078)

Above right: November 6, 1941 on maneuvers in North Carolina with the 9th Quartermaster Battalion. Well balanced, the 969/969As were often used without needing the side support jack; this Ford GP Jeep's 2,425 lb was not going to upset this one. (U.S. Army SC-130044)

Below: The 51st Ordnance Battalion is giving a Jeep a bath, with no need to deploy the stabilizing jacks to handle this featherweight. (U.S. Army SC-1832535)

Above: Fort Clark, Texas, June 19, 1942 with the 114th Ordnance Company. The superlative "Superman" was widely used when it came to the Diamond T wrecker truck; even those serious members in the photographic units in the Signal Corps did not hesitate to use it. (U.S. Army SC-175868)

Below: Frenchen, near Cologne, Germany, April 16, 1945. Inside a 3471st Ordnance Medium Automotive Company workshop, this Diamond T is going through its regular maintenance. To protect the truck and better guide the winch cable, its fender has been tripled in height, giving the vehicle an aggressive look. Not too visible at the rear, a metallic griddle meant that pushing and pulling could be done in safety. (Model 969, USA-0039927, contract no. W-398-QM-W-662.) (U.S. Army SC-345677)

DIAMOND T MODEL 969A WRECKER TRUCK PRODUCTION			
Quantities	**Orders**	**Registrations**	**Comments**
125	W-398-QM-10140 W-271-ORD-2792	004145 to 004269	93 taken on charge in 1941 & 32 taken on charge in 1942
250		006963 to 007212	All taken on charge in 1942
180	DA-W-398-QM-2	none	48 taken on charge in 1941 & 132 taken on charge in 1942
29	DA-W-398-QM-83	none	8 taken on charge in 1941 & 21 taken on charge in 1942
5	DA-W-398-Q-244	none	All taken on charge in 1942
150	W-398-QM-10889 W-271-ORD-2793	005916 to 006065	All taken on charge in 1942
1,314	W-398-QM-11509	008686 to 09999	All taken on charge in 1942
942	W-271-ORD-2537	0010000 to 0010941	90 taken on charge in 1942 & 852 taken on charge in 1943
1,594	W-398-QM-W-662	0038611 to 0040204	All taken on charge in 1943
1,537	W-271-ORD-2549	0077410 to 0078946	577 taken on charge in 1942 & 268 taken on charge in 1945 (& 692 non-acceptations)
371	W-271-ORD-2804	unknown	250 taken on charge in 1944 and 121 taken on charge in 1945
450	W-271-ORD-4577	0072815 to 0073264	None of this order was accepted
108	W-271-ORD-022-3739	0091518 to 0091625	All taken on charge in 1945.

June 13, 1945, Camp Brooklyn, southeast of Reims, the base whence U.S. troops were redeployed at the end of the war in Europe. What better than a Diamond T to repair a Diamond T. This is what S/Sgt Floyd N. Jordan, T/4 Carson N. Rogers, T/S Charles B. Rogers, and William D. Maxwell are doing. In less than six hours they had replaced the engine of a 969/696A so it could continue operations, or be sent to the Pacific. (U.S. Army SC-345688)

Left: The Saint Bernard of the communications and supply channels, Diamond T wreckers were present everywhere and helped out almost without fail. Either with their winch or cranes they extricated drivers from sticky situations like this Federal Model 94 x 43 semi-trailer tractor on a French road. (U.S. Army Signal Corps)

Below: Many accidents occurred along the roads of the Red Ball Express. In extremely trying conditions, the smallest mistake could turn into a tragedy. This GMC CCKW with its lost load of jerrycans is being righted without ceremony: the convoys had to get through with no time lost. (U.S. Army Signal Corps)

Right: Capturing the port at Antwerp in Belgium shortened supply lines thanks to the ABC route, though this did not mean that breakdowns and failures disappeared altogether. Broken-down vehicles were taken straight to repair workshops along the route. (U.S. Army Signal Corps)

Below: Another crucial route was the Ledo Road in Asia, where intense traffic issues were similar to those in Europe. With the power of its winch alone, this 969A easily righted a GMC CCKW which had tipped over onto its side. (U.S. Army Air Forces ref 74714 A.C.)

New Guinea, May 1944. Some 5,000 vehicles were assembled on this production line in the middle of the jungle. As the operation had no heavy lifting gear, Diamond Ts handled all the heavy work, like installing this wooden cargo body on the chassis of a GMC CCKW-252-A1. (Model 969A, USA-0010107, contract no. W-398-QM-11509.) (U.S. Army Signal Corps)

Utah Beach, June 11, 1944. LCT-522 (Landing Craft Tank) disembarks its load of vehicles. On the ramp, a Diamond T takes its place on a Rhino Ferry. Before the tarpaulin-covered cabin appeared, there was no antiaircraft mounting on the Diamond T. In the field, it was common for equipment on the GMCs to be recovered and adapted. Be they the M-32, M-36, or M-37 ring mounts, each model was worth recovering. (U.S. Navy)

Opposite top: Recovering equipment from the field was also part of the ordnance units' job. This wrecker towing a damaged 155-mm howitzer needs the help of a bulldozer to get out of the mud, near Dossenheim, northeast of Strasbourg. (U.S. Army SC-200867)

Opposite bottom: The rational use of issue equipment. On campaign, vehicles did not need a sheltered workshop for maintenance; everything was done in the field. It was much easier to carry out these operations with the nose in the air and without an inspection pit. (U.S. Army C-998)

Above: Demonstration by a Ward LaFrance at Camp Butner, September 24, 1943. All wreckers were equipped with these ground anchors used in a single or double line for all types of draught. (U.S. Army SC-168883)

Below: Normoyle, San Antonio, Texas. This configuration means that the two jibs must be opened out to 180° so that the transfer of the power is carried out in a straight line. The two ends of the jibs have to be aligned on the transversal axis formed by the gantry. (Private Collection)

THE DIAMOND T GANTRY: GENERAL USE

Right: The most important part of the Diamond T 969 was the gantry designed by the Ernest Holmes Company, designated Model W-45. With a nominal force of 5 tons for work in a straight line, its power could be doubled when the traction cable was reeved with a driven pulley.

1) Gearbox
2) Transfer axis
3) Winch drum
4) Compressor
5) Crane pulley
6) Boom pulley
7) Strut head
8) Cabling
9) Drive chain
10) Idler pulley
11) Control levers
12) Fire extinguisher
13) Strut extension pin
14) Strut
15) Tow bar
16) Equipment stowage boxes
(Source TM 10 1607)

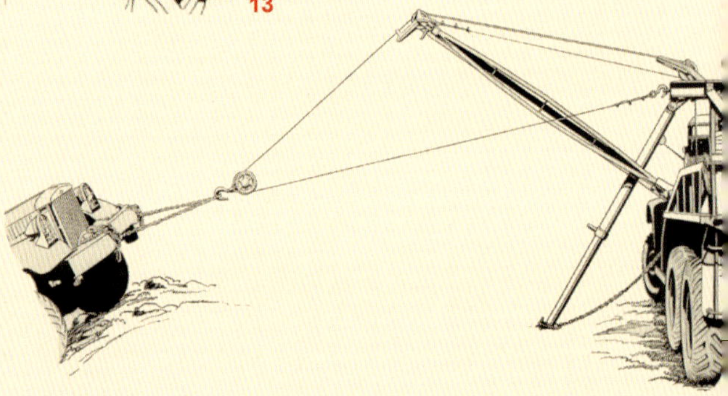

Above left: The primary use of the gantry was for winching with a single line (single line hook-up), directly from one of the gantry drums and by installing a bracing leg. Pivoting through 90° in relation to the longitudinal axis of the vehicle, the jib offered a work area of 180°. In this configuration all the power of the winch (5 tons) was used on a cable. (Source TM 10-1607)

Above right: The reeving technique on a strand (double line hook-up) enabled the power to be dispersed and the traction strength doubled without modifying the winch gears, through the intermediary of a pulley and a fixed point. This double line of traction increased breakdown possibilities of the Diamond T 969 from 5 tons to 10 tons. Using a strut, or even two, presupposed that the nature of the terrain would resist the hammering caused by the transfer of pressure on a reduced surface. (Source TM 10-1607)

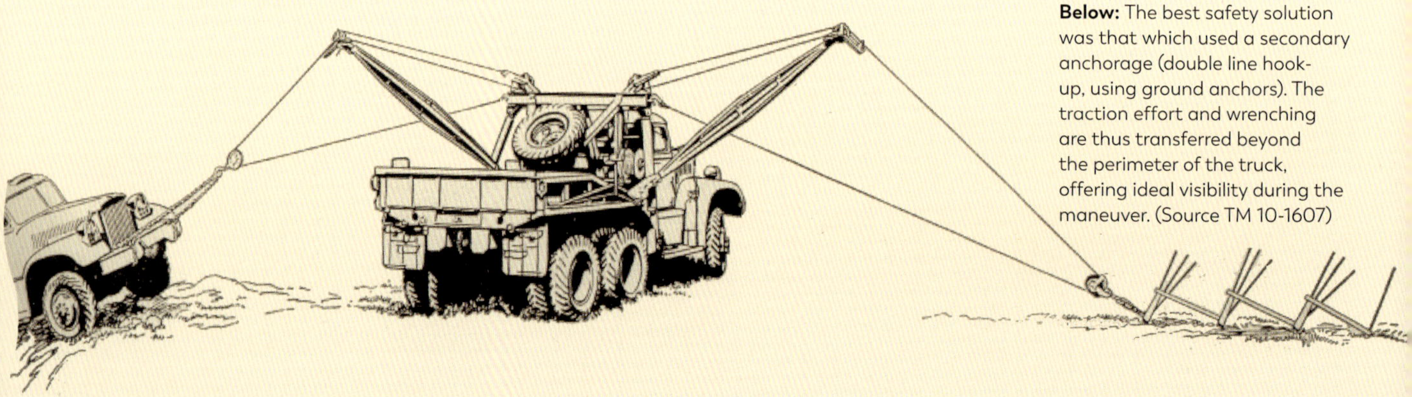

Below: The best safety solution was that which used a secondary anchorage (double line hook-up, using ground anchors). The traction effort and wrenching are thus transferred beyond the perimeter of the truck, offering ideal visibility during the maneuver. (Source TM 10-1607)

Left: Kwajalein Atoll, Marshall Islands, April 1944. Coming from Tarawa, taken several months earlier, this 969A tows a sterilization and treatment unit for drinking water; it is minus the protective grilles on its two headlamps. In this war in the back of beyond, the Army had its equipment deploy on an island-hopping basis, while infrastructure was established in the recently conquered territories. (U.S. Army Air Forces, ref 63487 A.C.)

Below: As well as the traditional onboard lot of tooling for the 4-ton, 6x6 trucks, the Diamond T wrecker was given a specific set of tools. (Source TM 10-1533)

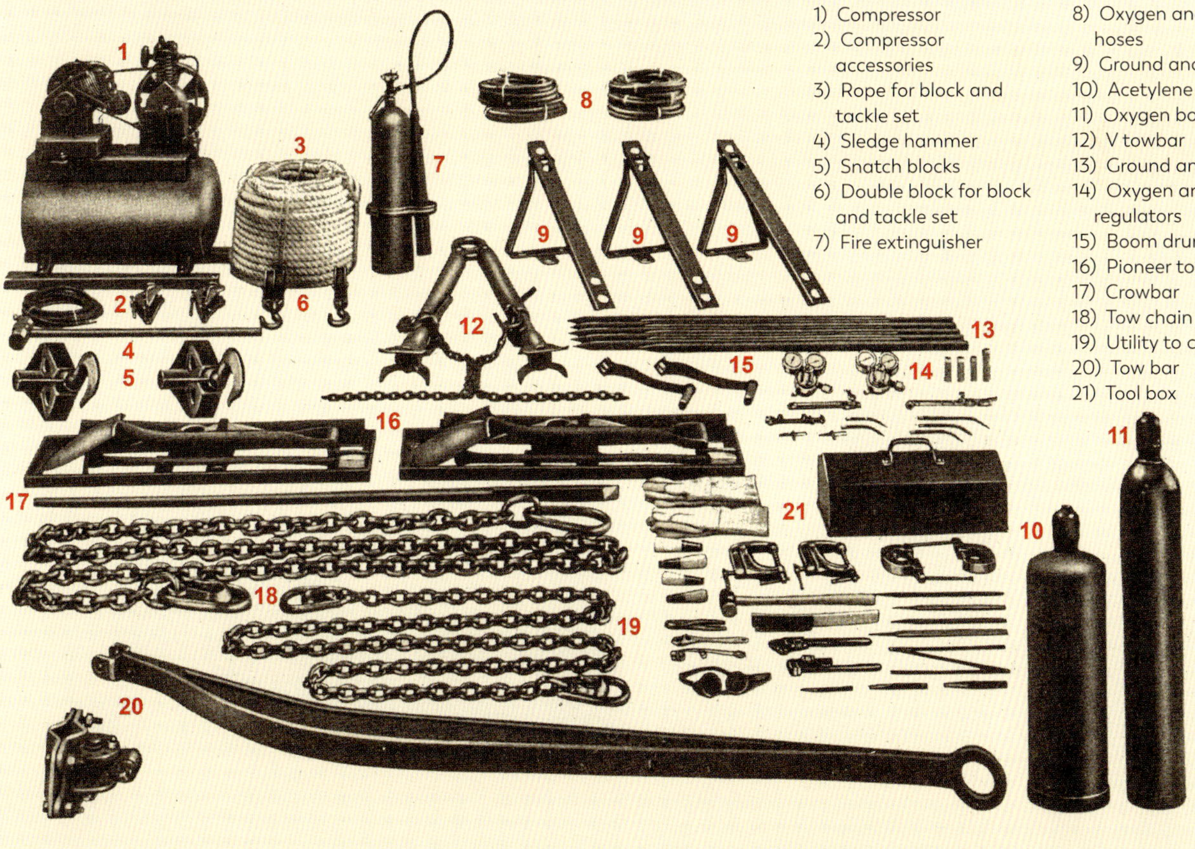

1) Compressor
2) Compressor accessories
3) Rope for block and tackle set
4) Sledge hammer
5) Snatch blocks
6) Double block for block and tackle set
7) Fire extinguisher
8) Oxygen and acetylene hoses
9) Ground anchors
10) Acetylene bottle
11) Oxygen bottle
12) V towbar
13) Ground anchor stakes
14) Oxygen and acetylene regulators
15) Boom drum cranks
16) Pioneer tool set
17) Crowbar
18) Tow chain
19) Utility to chain
20) Tow bar
21) Tool box

VILBISS COMPRESSOR

KELLOG COMPRESSOR

Above: Two companies provided the air compressors which equipped the Diamond T 969s: Vilbiss and Kellog. Power was from a small Briggs & Stratton Model N or WI single-cylinder block, which gave 150 psi. At the end of production, Kellog used a Johnson motor. The only official use of these compressors was for inflating tires during breakdowns. (Source TM 9-811)

Top: The tarpaulin-covered cabs were rarely appreciated by crews who had to wait long hours in all weather. They were regularly improved upon, and in the immediate postwar period, a lot of minor improvements in general—siren, double-tone horn, large work headlamps, and many others—were to be found. (Model 969, USA-0039821, contract no. W-398-QM-662.) (U.S. Army Signal Corps)

Above: Cali Norgeh Airport, Tehran, Iran, May 11, 1944. As a breakdown vehicle, the Diamond T 969 excelled in simple servicing tasks, like the transshipment of bombs. The rotation of the jibs, even partially, was a considerable asset. (U.S. Army SC-169509)

Below: Wrecker truck from the 17th Engineer Battalion, Fort Benning. The gantry on this breakdown truck has no work headlamps. (Model 969, USA-W-009321, contract no. W-398-QM-124027). (U.S. Army SC-124027)

7 Pontoon Trucks

A total of 144 Diamond T Model 970s and 576 Model 970As were ordered and taken on charge under the designation Ponton Truck. These were specific vehicles with a long wheelbase and an extended cargo body, intended only for the Corps of Engineers.

These pontoon (ponton in U.S. military parlance) trucks were not too different from the cargo truck Models 968s and 968As, except for their longer wheelbase which was increased from 151 inches to 172 inches. The mechanics remained exactly the same, except for the extension to the propeller shaft linking the transfer box to the rear differential, its length increasing like the wheelbase by 21 inches from 27½ inches to 48½ inches.

It was with the cargo body that the differences with the 968/968As were more visible. The two spare wheels were no longer fitted inside the cargo body but on a special mounting located on the chassis between the cab and the cargo body.

Right: There are no fewer than seven pontoon trucks in this image. They were also used for other tasks, like transporting pipeline sections. (U.S. Army Signal Corps)

Below: Registration no. USA-W-458486 for this Diamond T Model 970 from contract no. W-398-QM-8926, belonging to 72nd Engineer Ponton Battalion. Taken on charge in 1941, it has the off-road tires issued at the time, non-directional tires only appearing later. (U.S. Army Signal Corps)

DIAMOND T MODEL 970 PONTOON TRUCK PRODUCTION	
Chassis numbers 970-0001 to 970-0144 = 144 vehicles All tarpaulin-covered cabs from contract no. W-398-QM-8926 All taken on charge in 1941 and registered as follows:	(458235 to 458239) + (458476 to 458479) + (458482 to 458490) + (458495 to 458508) + (458510 to 458517) + (458519 to 458526) + (458804 to 458818) + (458797 to 458800) + (458842 to 458845) + (458995 to 458998) + 458211, 458218, 458227, 458232, 458233, 458241, 458242, 458248, 458251, 458256, 458258, 458268, 458269, 458274, 458279, 458283, 458289, 458294, 458298, 458301, 458306, 458311, 458316, 458319, 458321, 458322, 458326, 458327, 458329, 458334, 458337, 458348, 458354, 458377, 458397, 458398, 458436, 458467, 458471, 458473, 458474, 458492, 458802, 458820, 458827, 458836, 458838, 458840, 458847, 458849, 458857, 458861, 458865, 458873, 458879, 458887, 458951, 458952, 458958, 458967, 458974, 458976, 458983, 458985, 458987, 458990, 458992, 458993, 458493.

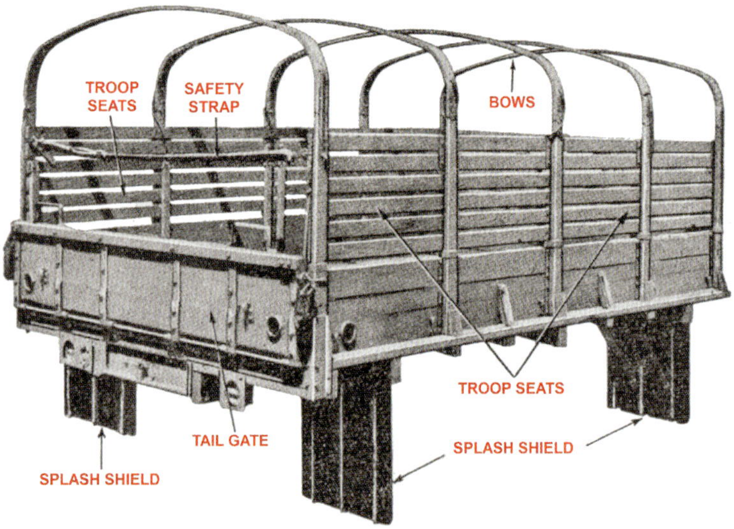

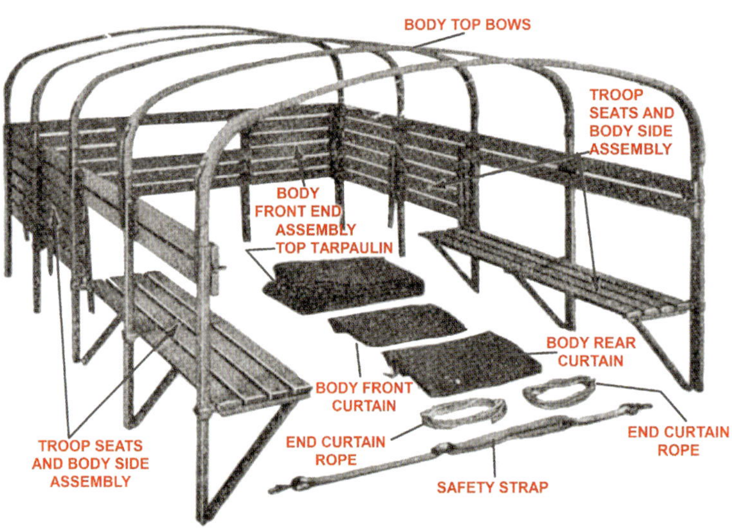

The benches built onto the side rails were the same length as the available space, since the two spare wheels had been repositioned for easier handling. So as to be able to modulate the interior, the benches were in two parts. The front part of the cargo body now being freed up, the side rail absent on the 968/968As was added.

The 970/970As were used to transport equipment and personnel and were specifically dedicated to the heavy ponton battalions in the Engineers, to work with the ponton tractor trucks, either Mack NJU-1s or Autocar U-8144-Ts. Their role was to transport the equipment which for one reason or another could not be carried by the 10- or 25-ton pontoon semi-trailer (Semi-Trailer, Ponton in military phraseology).

Three types of pontoon were in everyday use: the heavy ponton bridge, with a 25- to 40-ton capacity built on metal boats (heavy boats) each with a 25- to 30-ton capacity; the 10-ton small ponton bridge using boats (small boats), the freeboard of which was lower and which could take 5 to 8 tons each; and the 5-ton ponton bridge, the boats of which were pneumatic rafts. All these bridges were built depending on the cartage of the units having to cross them.

These pontoons could be placed in three different categories: firstly, the assault ponton which had to be set up quickly so as not to slow down the advancing combat units.

Left and above: The main element of the 970/970A, the all-wood cargo body will replace the all-metal one. Unlike the 968A, the manuals give no indication of when the change was made. (Source TM 9-811)

DIAMOND T MODEL 970A PONTOON TRUCK PRODUCTION			
Quantities	**Orders**	**Registrations**	**Comments**
7	W-398-QM-10140	482142 to 482148	All taken on charge in 1942
20	W-398-QM-10889	486898 to 486917	All taken on charge in 1942
343	W-398-QM-11509	4354739 to 4355081	174 units taken on charge in 1942 and 169 others in 1943
2	W-398-QM-W-662	4451067 to 4451068	All taken on charge in 1943 (wooden cargo body)
204		4558563 to 4558766	

Next was the combat support ponton, built either on floats or fixed abutments: the time taken to build it was not critical but as it was absolutely essential for establishing the lines of communication, it replaced an existing bridge which needed rebuilding.

Finally, there was the line-of-communications ponton bridge that replaced an irreparable existing bridge and which by circumstances became permanent, being built either on floats or fixed abutments.

The American Army jealously hung onto the 970/970As. Only nine examples were supplied to France as part of the Lend-Lease program.

Above: A common scene in Alaska on the Alcan Highway. Temporary floating bridges were used over the myriad rivers while waiting for fixed constructions. Here, as soon as it is finished, the sappers will be back to pick up their equipment which will be removed from the pontoon bridge using a Diamond T 970. (U.S. Army Signal Corps)

Above right: England, July 1944, a light ponton company heads for its embarkation port. The vehicles are loaded with parts that will make up the roadway for a floating bridge. The Diamond T 970/970As are towing 4-ton telephone construction and combination cable hauler trailers, the Signal companies' designation K-37. They are able to carry long equipment just as well as reels of telephone cable. (U.S. Army SC-169157)

Right: A typical wintry January in 1943 on a section of highway to Fairbanks, Alaska, where a convoy of Diamond T 970s has come across a local man and his sledge. The location of the two spare wheels typical of this model leaves no doubt as to its identity, being the only vehicle to carry them this way, just behind the cabin and no longer inside the cargo body. (Wirephoto ref. 70900)

Above: Registration no. USA-W-458887 for this Diamond T Model 970 from contract no. W-398-QM-8926 that has been paired up with a laboratory trailer from the Quartermaster Corps Mobile Petroleum Group at El Centro Naval Air Station in California. As the trailer design was all new, the truck has been given the task of bringing it through the desert to undergo its air-conditioning, insulation, and generator tests. (U.S. Army SC-348496)

Left: Without its cargo box, this Model 970 shows the double spare wheel support on the chassis leaning against the cab. The long wheelbase leaves no doubt as to its purpose as a pontoon truck.

Below: Negotiating a wooden bridge with some difficulty, this 970/970A is towing a 25-ton pontoon semi-trailer with two metal floats for a temporary bridge. The trailer was normally hitched to a Mack NJU-1 or an Autocar U-8144-T, and using a two-wheel ponton dolly was therefore indispensable in moving such equipment. (U.S. Army Signal Corps)

8

Dump Truck

A single-task special version, the Diamond T Model 972, with 9,922 examples taken on charge by the Army, was the construction units' biggest dumping vehicle. With its 151-inch wheelbase, it was derived directly from the Model 968A cargo truck.

Up until 1943, surprisingly, only small-sized dump trucks were to be found in the American Army classifications. Two models shared the dumping jobs: the Chevrolet 4x4, 1½-ton and the GMC 6x6, 2½-ton dump trucks.

These trucks carried a double designation: transport and dumping—cargo dump trucks—and although at the time they were more or less suited to the work of a campaigning army, in conditions with a paucity of infrastructure, they quickly proved inadequate to carry out large-scale work. Before being used by the Corps of Engineers, fitted or not with a winch, the Chevrolet's first job was to supply the cavalry stables with fodder and remove the waste. Because of the chassis limitations, the GMC CCKW-353 could not utilize the whole surface of its dump skip which had had to be reduced by a good quarter of its surface by fitting a safety panel.

Above: In the town of Furth in Germany, a few miles from Nuremberg, the 834th Aviation Engineer Battalion is clearing rubble following Allied air raids. Registered as USA-4451789, this example without a winch was part of a series not classified as such. (U.S. Army Air Forces, ref 76685 A.C.)

Left: Photographed from another angle, the scene shows the extent of the damage. While a D7 bulldozer creates a mountain of rubble, a crane with a bucket is loading up the Diamond T. (U.S. Army Air Forces, ref 76694 A.C.)

Right: 104th Engineer Combat Battalion, Okinawa, April 29, 1945. This view of a CCKW-353 shows how limited its load was with the special separation on the trailer. Behind it the Diamond T 972 has no need of one.

Below: 834th Aviation Engineer Battalion, Saint-Pierre-du-Mont, Normandy, July 1944. Flanked by two GMC CCKW 353s, a Diamond T 972 tips its load. The differences are obvious, from the quantity of earth carried to the size of the cab protector. (U.S. Army Signal Corps)

When it became necessary to create an extensive infrastructure in an inhospitable environment to satisfy the U.S. Army Air Forces' needs of new airbases on the way to Japan, it was no longer a question of relying on the smaller Chevrolets and GMCs. The Pacific islands were not simply sandy or stony atolls: establishing bases for the fleets of USAAF bombers required millions of cubic meters of rubble of all sorts to be displaced and astronomical quantities of metaling stones to be brought in for laying runway foundations.

Only a vehicle specifically designed for the job would be able to carry out these titanic tasks properly. In Europe, the fighting left towns and villages ravaged, with vast piles of rubble that had to be removed or displaced. It was the Corps of Engineers who took up the challenge but they needed a suitable vehicle.

Production

Diamond T 972 production seems to have been chaotic considering the official documents emanating from the various authorities assigned to compile all the orders/production/taking-on-charge data. The bottom line is that 9,000 vehicles with the 4-ton, 6x6 dump truck shape were built by Diamond T. In this production, some vehicles were delivered without a winch and it is still impossible to say how many; some documents mention 1,410 and others 3,427. What is certain is that, given the various photographic reports, the truth lies somewhere between the two figures. In 1944, 922 Diamond T 968A cargo trucks were diverted from their intended usage to become dump trucks with a winch, which fixed total production of these dump trucks at 9,922 units.

Production was spread over the period from February 1943 when the four first examples were taken on charge, to August 1945 when production ceased with the last 367 vehicles. Within the context of supplies provided to the Allies, only 39 Diamond T 972s were supplied—20 to the USSR and 19 to France, all with winches.

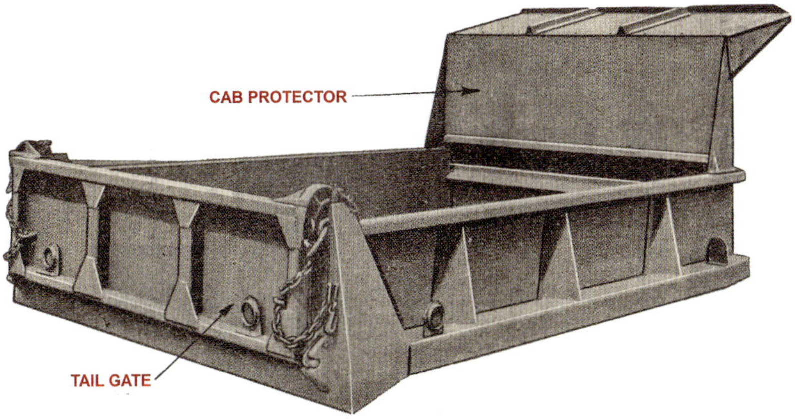

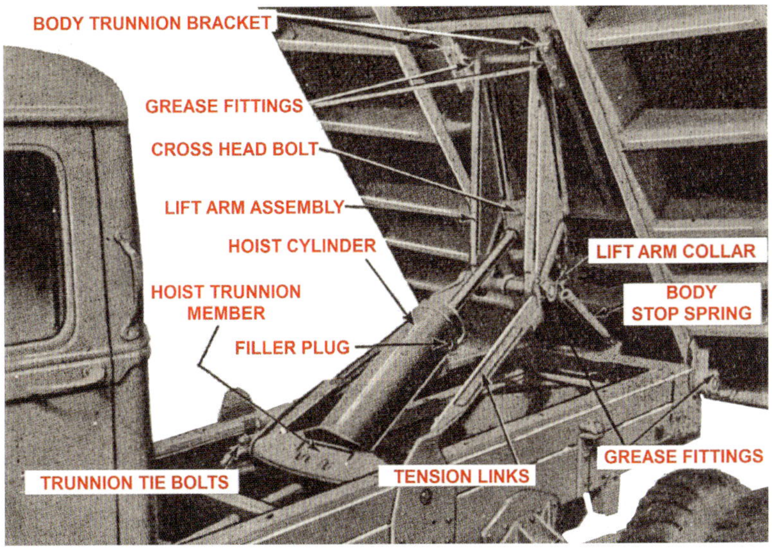

Top: The impressive body of the Diamond T 972 was made wholly of steel with a large, removable cab protector, built by the Gallon Allsteel Body Company. (Extract from TM 9-811)

Above: The leverage mechanism came from the Gar Wood Company. As with the skip, it was set up on a chassis subframe fitted onto the truck chassis. (Extract from TM 9-811)

DIAMOND T MODEL 972 DUMP TRUCK PRODUCTION

Quantities	Orders	Registrations	Comments
1,017	W-398-QM-W-662 W-271-ORD-2549	4451069 to 4452085	All taken on charge in 1943
187		4459169 to 4459355	All taken on charge in 1943
1,410		4459356 to 4460765	206 taken on charge in 1943 and 1,204 taken on charge in 1944 (all w/out winch).
488	W-271-ORD-4577	4555515 to 4556002	All taken on charge in 1944
356	W-271-ORD-11-022-240	4596689 to 4597044	All taken on charge in 1944.
843	W-271-ORD-11-022-289	4598203 to 4509945	All taken on charge in 1944
1,275		4770084 to 4771358	435 taken on charge in 1944 and 840 taken on charge in 1945.
2,181		4773875 to 4776055	All taken on charge in 1945
436	W-271-ORD-11-022-3739	4797950 to 4798385	All taken on charge in 1945
196		4835777 to 4835972	All taken on charge in 1945
611		4835975 to 4836585	All taken on charge in 1945
922	W-271-ORD-11-022-289	4607260 to 4608406	Diamond T 968As converted to 972s. Series of 1,147 numbers out of which the 922 registration numbers used were taken. All taken on charge in 1945

Above: Making the runways on Guam in the Marianas required vast quantities of asphalt as the production units operated night and day. An unending stream of Diamond T 972s was given the job of supplying the spreaders non-stop. (U.S. Army Air Forces ref. 56662 A.C.)

Right: Without all these units at the rear, carrying on the fight would have very quickly become impossible. These men in the shadows were not there to fight: their mission was to provide unfailing logistic support. (U.S. Army Air Forces ref. 64658 A.C.)

The only way of protecting the skip from the bitumen sticking to it was to daub it with fuel oil. To get rid of the surplus, the drivers just let it drain away by tipping the skips. (U.S. Army Air Forces ref. 64658 A.C.)

The Shape

The Diamond T 972 was mounted on the same base as all the brand's 6x6, 4-ton vehicles, with a short 151-inch wheelbase. It was its rear technical section that was special in that it consisted of a dump skip, made of steel, with a volume of 4 cubic yards. Unlike all the other dump trucks in the U.S. Army which had a rear section that could also be used for transporting personnel, the 972's body was intended for one use only and had neither side rails nor benches. Made by Gallon Allsteel Body Co., Ohio, the skip was surmounted by an imposing removable cab protector; its hydraulic parts were made by the Gar Wood Company. There were several designs used for the cab protector; the part covering the truck cab was at first made of sheet metal reinforced by metal nervures, then covered with a layer of wood to improve and increase the deadening effect on the bumps.

Two levers in the cabin operated the dump skip. From the transfer gearbox, the first lever controlled the movement of a shaft with universal joints linked to a hydraulic pump which put the oil circuit under pressure so that the hydraulic jack would function, lifting the skip. The second, with its three positions, began lifting, under pressure from the pump: in the intermediary position, it stopped the jack moving whilst keeping the skip at the angle required, and the third, once the gearbox was declutched, enabled the hydraulic liquid to flow back under the effect of gravity and the weight of the skip, which then came back to its original position.

Tilting only lengthways, the skip swung up on the rear hinges linking it to the sub-assembly frame which bore the whole weight of the installation. The rear tailgate swung on two axes: in the normal manner on its lower axis, or by activating a lever situated on the left of the forward face of the skip, making it swing along its upper axis only. On the late-production Diamond T 972s, an alarm warned the driver that the PTO feeding the hydraulic pump was still engaged whilst the truck was moving.

The vehicle's external accessories had to be specially organized because the vehicle was compact and only used for one function, meaning that the single spare wheel and two jerrycan holders were installed on the front side of the skip between it and the rear of the cab.

As with most military vehicles of the period, the Diamond T 972 had its administrative quirks. If one refers to the different versions of the technical manuals, all these trucks with a dump skip came off the production line with an all-metal cab. If administratively the situation is clear, the reality

is quite different since a number of photographs clearly show dump trucks with a tarpaulin-covered cab. Nothing can explain this difference between the technical manual and the reality in the field.

Use

With this special dump skip, the Diamond T 972 rarely ventured from its comfort zone, being used for little else except carrying all sorts of aggregates. Its configuration ensured it had a long shelf life. Even in the mid-1950s, it was still indexed as a standard vehicle in the American classifications. It was also unique because it appeared in two different classifications: road and off-road vehicles.

Above and left: The 805th Aviation Engineer Battalion at work in the Marianas, October 1944. The aerodrome installations were not finished when the U.S. Army Air Forces took possession of the runways. Here a loaded Diamond T 972 gives way to two Republic P-47 Thunderbolts taking off on a mission. (U.S. Army Air Forces, ref 63983 and 64443 A.C.)

Above: Okinawa, May 1945, the 1878th Aviation Engineer Battalion on the move. The vehicles are overloaded beyond reason but to ensure nothing is lost, the vehicles have been allocated makeshift tarpaulins to keep everything in. (U.S. Army Air Forces, ref 64635 A.C.)

Below: Guam, in the Marianas. Be they GMC CCKW-353s or Diamond T 972s, the dump truck versions were inseparable and worked alongside each other in the same units. (U.S. Army Air Forces, ref 64417 A.C.)

Left: Work in the Marianas took its toll on both men and vehicles more quickly than envisaged. It was mainly the tires and the suspension that suffered from the type of terrain. It was not uncommon for 50–60% of a unit's pool to be out of action because of this. The vehicles most in need of repair and awaiting spares from the Ordnance Department were put on blocks so others could be repaired in the interim. (U.S. Army Air Forces, ref A-39130)

Left: Building Isely Field, Saipan, August 1944. This example from the 963rd Aviation Engineer Battalion is emptying its load of stones for a runway's foundations. The cab protector was not an absolute necessity and its absence did not prevent the truck from being used. It was up to the crane operator not to fill the skip too far forward. (U.S. Army Air Forces, ref 53006 A.C.)

Below: Ryuryu Retto, Okinawa, May 1945. The monsoon rains left a quagmire. Despite the Diamond T's agility, getting rid of the huge quantities of mud accumulated on the running gear was an issue. The cab protector had to regularly be repaired and reinforced and it was common for steel reinforcements to be added to strengthen the corners between the vertical and sloping parts, like on this truck from the 1878th Aviation Engineer Battalion. (U.S. Army Air Forces, ref 65058 A.C.)

Above: Recovering enemy equipment for transfer to the United States was preoccupying, but enabled the materiel to be evaluated in depth and any important information sent back to the front. On Saipan, August 8, 1944, the 804th Aviation Engineer Battalion recovers Mitsubishi A6M Zeroes which are placed on and fastened to 20-ton, flatbed trailers, towed by 972s. (U.S. Army Air Forces, ref 63375 A.C.)

Right: The 364th Fighter Group of the 67th Fighter Wing at Slater F-375 airfield, Eighth Air Force, Honnington, England. Repairing damage to one of the runways, one of the Federal 606 Type 2 trucks lifts part of the pierced steel plating (PSP), while the men fill in the gaps with aggregates carried by the Diamond T 972. (U.S. Army Air Forces, ref A-72075 A.C.)

This characteristic was interesting because it officially allowed load ratings and towing capabilities to be adapted to the nature of the terrain. This applied particularly to the firm ground of the volcanic islands in the Pacific, but it did mean that tire lifespan was shortened, since they suffered on the sharp metaling of the runway foundations at the new airbases.

Right: Seventh Air Force on the island of Saipan, in the Marianas. The 804th Aviation Engineer Battalion is lengthening the Aslito airfield runway with the help of PSP. This 972 is in its basic configuration without a winch at the front. (U.S. Army Air Forces, ref 63735 A.C.)

Above: A heightened skip and a search lamp installed on the roof of the cab, together with camouflage netting on the top of the cab protector, are this example's particularities. (Private Collection)

Above right: The Diamond T 6x6, 4-ton trucks' incredible endurance allowed them to carry loads well over the permitted theoretical limits. Increasing the volume by heightening the skip sides with DIY panels was not uncommon. Piercing a rearview window in the cab protector was also one of the modifications noted. (Private Collection)

Right: Small modifications were common on this type of vehicle, like changing the lighting so as to have only blackout lights to avoid the untimely use of the road lights at night. Nicknames were also common, like *Miss Maria* on this one. (Private Collection)

A new airfield in the Aleutians"—typical service of Diamond T 6 x 6 Army trucks

New Nests for the Eagle's Brood!

A TINY new speck appears on the war-maps—a brief sentence in some cautiously worded communique—"*From new bases* our aircraft attacked enemy concentrations at ________." That's all, but it means that army engineers with American trucks have clawed another airfield out of the frozen tundra or steaming jungle. And what a difference each new nesting place can make to our gallant youngsters who wear the eagle's silver wings!

Thousands of trucks—unfailing, rugged Diamond T "prime-movers," driving through three massive live axles to ten giant-tired wheels—must lug countless loads of earth, rock and cement to make these prayed-for landing fields. Built into those trucks, into every Super-Service Diamond T engine—every frame and drive member—sweated home with every rivet and bolt—welded into every seam—is the spirit of Diamond T craftsmen, brothers-in-arms to the fighting men they are serving.

BUY WAR BONDS FOR VICTORY
—THEY WILL PAY YOU
WITH INTEREST... AND LIBERTY

Building war vehicles is our task today. Tomorrow, when Victory has been earned, Diamond T will present to business men the wide world over, new and still finer versions of Diamond T Super-Service Trucks to serve the world they have helped to save.

DIAMOND T MOTOR CAR CO., CHICAGO
Established 1905

★ DIAMOND T MOTOR TRUCKS ★

9 Canadian Trucks

These 975/975As were unique as they were the result of a purchase by an Allied country. In 1940, the payload per truck of the Canadian Army's fleet did not exceed 3 tons and with the start of the war, Canada did not have time to undertake any special studies.

The country's industry had to run at full speed and concentrate on existing models. Nonetheless, the need was there, especially where workshop trucks and heavy goods vehicles were concerned. The Canadians found what they were looking for south of the border and more particularly in the 4-ton, 6x6 truck range which Diamond T had started producing for military purposes.

Left: Lorry, 4-ton, 6-wheel, Crane Mark VI. The movement of the crane and the hook was controlled by a different electric motor. (Canadian Army)

Below: Lorry, 4-ton, 6-wheel, Machinery Type H, for this Diamond T 975. The technical body specific to this model was identifiable by the presence of double access panels along the front half of the side. So that this super-long wheelbase could be operated mechanically, the rear propeller shaft was in two parts. The vehicle's primary use was as a steel-working field workshop. (Canadian Army)

Although the shape, the mechanics, and performance were particularly suitable, they were too small; the Canadians wanted the length of the chassis and the wheelbase to be modified. The Americans were not overly forthcoming but allowed the Diamond T/ Canada partnership to develop on the basis of a 201-inch wheelbase, or 30 inches longer than the 970/970As, meaning that the side members had to be lengthened and an extra traverse installed, increasing these from six to seven.

A total of 307 examples of these chassis-type vehicles were supplied, under the designation 975, with chassis numbers 975-0165 to 975-0307, and with a tarpaulin-covered cab. Also supplied were 811 Model 975As, with chassis numbers 975A-0676 to 975A-811, also with an open cab.

Canada used them under eight different designations with many changes to the bodies:

- Lorry, 4-ton, 6-wheel Crane Mark VI had a crane pivoting through 360° made by Coles, the English company, with an electric motor. Its strength was 3 tons at 17 feet.
- Lorry, 4-ton, 6-wheel Crane Mark VII was similar to the above but the crane was a Bay City Model 10 and worked with a 46-hp gasoline engine. Its strength was between 4,480 lb at 8 feet and 2,240 lb at 13 feet.
- Lorry, 4-ton, 6-wheel FBE (Folding Boat Equipment) was fitted with an adjustable structure

Above: This Diamond T is coupled to a trailer which is also part of the workshop that consists of an electric generator and a 60-ton press, among other things. (Canadian Army)

Below: This Lorry, 4-ton, 6-wheel Machinery Type M is a field workshop truck for mechanical repairs. Its steel body is 15 feet long and has a large work surface. (Canadian Army)

for carrying three barges used in building floating bridges.

- Lorry, 4-ton, 6-wheel GS (General Service) was a cargo version with a high steel body, used for transporting elements like Bailey bridges.
- Lorry, 4-ton, 6-wheel Machinery Type H was a workshop lorry designed using initially a tarpaulin-covered metal body with a double access door on each side.
- Lorry, 4-ton, 6-wheel Machinery Type M was a workshop lorry with an entirely rigid body.
- Lorry, 4-ton, 6-wheel Machinery Type RE-25KW was identical outside to the Type H but the workshop had a gantry with a handling hoist.
- Lorry, 4-ton, 6-wheel Pontoon had a superstructure for transporting rigid elements of the floating bridges and Bailey bridges.

Left: Lorry, 4-ton, 6-wheel GS, with its typical metal cargo body. Men from a bridge company of the Royal Canadian Army Service Corps (RCASC) load the structural elements of a Bailey bridge. (Canadian Army)

Below: Lorry, 4-ton, 6-wheel Pontoon and its special structure for transporting the rigid parts of floating bridges or elements of the Bailey bridge aprons. This version differed from the FBE model by the single equipment case on its left-hand side. (Canadian Army)

Above: Lorry, 4-ton, 6-wheel FBE was very similar to the pontoon version, but had more equipment cases and its structure was slightly different. Whatever the model, Pontoon or FBE, the technical part was self-standing; it was 192 inches long x 94 inches wide x 91 inches high, above the vehicle chassis. Of all the Diamond T range, this configuration made it the longest truck with a total length of 323 inches (26 feet 11 inches) and height of 136 inches (11 feet 4 inches). (Canadian Army)

Below: Late 1944 somewhere in Holland, an RCASC convoy has stopped; the last three vehicles are Diamond T 975s of the Lorry, 4-ton, 6-wheel GS type. The layout of the cargo body shows that it is really an equipment transport and has no benches or side rails for carrying personnel. (Canadian Army)

10 The Bare Chassis

The bare chassis category of Diamond Ts ordered from the factory, without any fixtures and fittings on the technical rear section, remains something of an administrative mystery.

A total of 2,499 Diamond Ts in the bare chassis version were taken on charge in four different models. Whether the cab was all-metal or tarpaulin-covered, they all went to different fitters whose task it was to fit out the chassis with special equipment. (Source SNL G-509)

According to the tables of the allocation of administrative and technical vehicle registration numbers, they all bore the designation Model 968A, short or long wheelbase, with or without a winch.

This classification went against all that had been set up, whatever the orders were to the majority of the army suppliers. Unlike other army suppliers, the Chicago firm, confusingly, regrouped four new sub-categories which were quite distinct under a designation that was already in use.

The designation 968A attributed to the cargo truck version with a 151-inch wheelbase was also used for the bare chassis with a long wheelbase and with or without a winch. Yet some of these vehicles were also related to the Diamond T 972s or 970As.

In its Summary Report of Acceptance, the Ordnance Department listed 2,197 vehicles without any fixtures and fittings on the rear technical part: 1,181 units with a short wheelbase and a winch, 295 with a short chassis without a winch, 583 with a long chassis and a 172-inch wheelbase with a winch, and 138 with a long chassis but without a winch.

Following the Lend-Lease report, none of these vehicles appears in the deliveries made to Allied countries, the American Army keeping them for its own use. The short-chassis vehicles with a winch were easily identifiable in the vast range of special technical fittings, the 800-gallon bituminous distributor tank, the 800-gallon asphalt distributor tank, the 1,000-gallon water distributor tank, and the M1 swinging boom crane (or in military parlance, Crane Swinging Boom M1) being the most common models. The long chassis with a winch was used as the basis for three conversions: the oil field body, the tractor trucks and the map reproduction equipment trucks.

The Chassis Without a Winch

Of the few examples supplied, 433 units were lost in the reports and the statistics of the Army, and an undefined number were used as snow plows. The lack of a winch on the truck front enabled different types of blades to be supplied and installed—for example, by William Bros., with its Model AH Snoflyer V-Blade, or the Model 23 Straight-Blade with a side blade by Bruch/Ross. The Rotary Snow-Plow was also mounted on these bare chassis; the independent machinery installed behind the cab was built by William Bros. or by Klauer Manufacturing. But one must not draw too many conclusions from this. Many photographs show us that versions without a winch had no front fenders, which differed from the version with a winch. Versions were only distinguishable by having a winch and its mechanism, or not. This was valid for all the types of trucks indexed under the reference "Chassis with Cab," or "Truck, No Body."

ORDERS/TAKING ON CHARGE OF BARE CHASSIS VEHICLES			
Orders	**Date**	**Registration**	**Number**
151-in Wheelbase Short-Chassis with Winch, 4-ton, 6x6 Diamond T Model 968A Truck			
W-398-QM-10140	1941	461247 + 461248 + 461251 + 461253 + 461255 + 461256 + 461258 + 461262 + 461358 + (461528 to 461537) + (482130 to 482141)	31 examples
W-398-QM-10889	1942	Without known registration number	16 examples
W-398-QM-11509	1942	4111269 + 4111274 + 4111275 + (4111151 to 4111153) + (4111328 to 4111342) and 84 units w/out known registration number	105 examples
W-271-ORD-4577	1944	(4558040 to 4558188)	149 examples
W-271-ORD-2549	1943	(4558254 to 4558562)	309 examples
W-271-ORD-11-022-240	1944	(4596520 to 4596688)	169 examples
W-271-ORD-11-022-3739	1945	(4597045 to 4597605) 159 vehicles cancelled	402 examples
151-inch Wheelbase Short-Chassis without Winch, 4-ton, 6x6 Diamond T Model 968A Truck			
W-271-ORD-11-022-289	1944	(4605171 to 4605425)	255 examples
W-271-ORD-11-022-289	1944	Without known registration number	40 examples
172-inch Wheelbase Long Chassis with Winch, 4-ton, 6x6 Diamond T Model 968A Truck			
W-398-QM-W-662	1942	(4450943 to 4451066) + (4558252 to 4558253)	126 examples
W-271-ORD-4577	1944	(4558189 to 4558251)	63 examples
W-271-ORD-11-022-3739	1944	(4597606 to 4597842) 28 vehicles cancelled	209 examples
W-271-ORD-11-022-289	1945	(4597917 to 4598202) 101 vehicles cancelled	185 examples
172-inch Wheelbase Long Chassis without Winch, 4-ton, 6x6 Diamond T Model 968A Truck			
W-271-ORD-11-022-3739	1944	Without known registration number	96 examples
W-271-ORD-11-022-289	1944	(4599078 to 4599133) 14 vehicles cancelled	42 examples

Distributor, Water Truck-Mounted

According to the Technical Manual 5-1150 definition, the full designation was Distributor, Water Truck-Mounted, 1,000 gal., Rosco Model NME (or 1,000-gallon Rosco Model NME, truck-mounted, water distributor in normal English). It was designed for the controlled sprinkling of a predetermined quantity of water for stabilizing the ground over a large area so as to provide an optimal humidity content.

As it happens, the vehicle was also designed with its low-pressure system, for sprinkling water over dust on the ground. It was also used for transporting low-viscosity liquids or water (not drinking water), and as an extra water-supply vehicle in the case of a fire. Entirely self-contained, because of its various functions, the vehicle was designed for sucking up water, draining, drying, bailing out barges or embarkations, and even as a fire truck using its soft pipes as fire hoses.

Rosco of Minneapolis supplied and installed its Model MME machinery on the short 151-inch wheelbase Diamond T chassis. It was made up principally of a platform with an electrically welded elliptical steel tank holding 1,000 gallons, a Gorman-Rupp Model 30M centrifugal pump, and all the piping needed for transferring liquids. Working

Above: The water-spraying truck was one of the particularities of the U.S. Army, like all vehicles made on the Diamond T 968A chassis. Its tank held more than 977 gallons. (Source TM 5-1150)

independently using a 1,506-cc (91.9-cubic inch) Wisconsin VE-41 gasoline engine rated at 2,200 rpm, the MME model had a rear foldable and extendable 24-feet boom for spraying.

It was a compact vehicle where only the rear piping protruded beyond the truck's outer dimensions and was the Engineers' standard vehicle, though they only ordered 105 examples.

Right: In the midst of the 1189th Engineer Base Depot in Hollandia, New Guinea, five 1,000-gallon water tank distributors await their next assignment, May 1945. The first of the group still has all its seagoing protection, applied before leaving the U.S. (U.S. Army SC-313863)

Easily identified by the two steps at the rear of its sides, here it is in its road configuration with the spraying arms folded back entirely. (Source TM 5-1150)

Hampton Roads Port of Embarkation. This water sprayer has been loaded and secured on a flatbed wagon before proceeding to the dockside. It has been prepared for a sea voyage with only the more fragile parts still requiring protection. (U.S. Army Signal Corps)

Farther along, the vehicle has reached the port and is now ready to be loaded aboard ship. Light panels have been affixed and fastened to the glasswork and the radiators, thus completing its temporary mothballing. (U.S. Army Signal Corps)

Loaded without much ado, just with side beams to prevent the bodywork from folding up, the truck is off to the Pacific islands. Note that this example, despite its lengthened chassis extended forward and with its special fender, has neither winch nor mechanism. (U.S. Army Signal Corps)

Unfortunately, these trucks were only available in small numbers and could not carry out all the spraying jobs that had to be done by themselves. Though vehicles and trailers intended for supplying drinking water—like the 700-gallon GMC CCKW-353 water tank trucks or the 1,500-gallon water tank semi-trailers—were modified by installing spraying lines, at times in the field other sophisticated means of replacing the Diamond T model were used.

Saipan, Mariana Islands. The water-spraying Diamond T 972s were delivered to units building the airbases in order to reduce the inevitable clouds of dust. Made with DIY means using simple sheet metal, the tanks were used only for carrying water. They therefore had no apparatus of any sort, or any sophisticated outlets, just an opening on the upper surface for filling and pumping. There was only one restriction for the water type: it could not have any material suspended in it, like salt, as it would clog up the spray jets. (U.S. Army Air Forces ref. 641228-A.C.)

Left: Anguar Island in the Carolinas, October 4, 1944. Using materials meant for other jobs was the solution the 1884th Aviation Engineer Battalion of the Seventh Air Force found in its struggle against the dust. Here, once again, a Diamond T 972 is being used as a simple towing vehicle for this trailer that is normally used to produce hot water. In the absence of any apparatus, spraying was done by gravity from the drain opening, controlled by a man balancing on the back. (U.S. Army Air Forces ref. 70647-A.C.)

Left: Normandy, summer 1944, a unit of the IX Engineer Command of the Ninth Air Force has solved the problem of the lack of a specific vehicle for spraying water on a runway under construction: a Diamond T 972 is equipped with a makeshift tank, towing a pump installed on a wheeled chassis and fitted with a large spray boom. Pumping was done by inserting a soft pipe into the tank, with gravity doing the rest. This operation was vital for stabilizing the ground, stripped as it was of its topsoil. (U.S. Army Signal Corps)

Swinging Boom Crane Truck M

Rarely has such a specific vehicle been ordered for a single use: lifting and handling the Chemical Warfare Service's Type A or D 4-ton container.

Using the 151-inch-wheelbase Diamond T 968A as a basis, the vehicle had a rear metal platform and a central lifting gantry. This equipment consisted mainly of a lifting arm fitted on a mast, installed directly on the truck chassis, just behind the cab. To make sure the truck did not tip over sideways when the boom was swiveled, a stabilizing jack on either side, on extendable arms, was fitted. Stabilizing lengthways was obtained by two stabilizers fitted at the rear of the chassis. To avoid the tower twisting and folding, it was supported by two tautening struts, connecting it to the front fender.

Operated by a standard PTO engaged inside the cabin, the lifting gantry with a double winch was operated using three large levers and an engine rpm control gauge, all these fitted directly to the crane. The first winch controlled the jib's vertical movements and the second the handling of the loads to be lifted or lowered. Made by the Winch & Crane Division of Gar Wood Industries, Inc., it had two work positions.

The jib could be positioned manually, with lengths of 13 feet or 20 feet, giving it a maximum capacity of 5,200 lb (at 13 feet) and 3,600 lb (at 20 feet) depending on the angle. A reinforced version with 15- or 20-feet working lengths appeared later, with a maximum capacity of 9,000 lb and 10,900 lb.

Above: The Swinging Boom Crane Truck M1 was an isolated example among the range of vehicles based on a bare chassis. Although all the others were made for the Engineers, this one was for the use of the Chemical Warfare Service only. This group of photographs enables one to appreciate the position of the boom when transported, then with the crane boom slightly extended, and finally with the jib fully extended. (Source TM 5-1150)

It was not common to see the Chemical Warfare Service's three main special vehicles all together: an M1 Diamond T 968A swinging boom crane truck, an M2 chemical handling trailer, and an M1 GMC CCKW-353 chemical service truck. When extended as far as possible, the jib of the Diamond T was 240 inches long and could easily lift chemical containers. Empty, these weighed around 1,322 lb, for a payload of 1,885 lb. They were mainly used for transporting combat gas like phosgene, chlorine, or chloropicrin. (U.S. Army Signal Corps)

Above: This example of an M1 968a swinging boom crane truck is quite bogged down in the sand and will not get out on its own. With its 100 registration no. USA-W-461537, it was part of the first order of bare chassis Diamond Ts, contract no. W-398-QM-10140 which was only for 31 units. (Private Collection)

Left: The bracing hook and wires of the tower was this model's particularity. The length of the jib together with the weights of the loads to be lifted and the particular way the crane was fixed to the chassis necessitated this precaution to avoid it tipping over and ripping the bottom out of the vehicle. (Private Collection)

Above: Two versions of technical body were available, like this one with only one side window; this identifies the truck as a Camera Section truck for photographic reproduction, serving with the Third Air Force in the U.S. (Private Collection)

Below: The second type of truck has two side windows for all sorts of impressions on paper, in the case of this Press Section truck. When the rotary press was in action, 14,000 sheets could be printed in an hour. The 657th Topographic Battalion of the First Army has camouflaged its vehicles by positioning them along a hedge near Eupen in Belgium, October 1944. (Private Collection)

Map Reproduction Truck

The map reproduction trucks were a large family using mainly semi-trailers, seven sorts of GMC CCKW-353s, and three models of 172-inch wheelbase long-chassis Diamond T 968As, which all used a unique technical body. Together they formed a line producing and reproducing mapping documents from photographic installations. They were also able to work as simple field printers.

Built by various companies like Peter Wendel & Sons, Inc., or McCabe Powers Autobody Co., the technical bodies of these trucks were specific in that they could be organized by extending the rear doors and the panels forming the roof, sides, and rear.

Apparently identical from the outside, they differed in how the windows were positioned, a corbeled gantry above the vehicle cab that enabled different configurations to be used like the position of the spare wheel, and the fixation of the skein winders for the cabling and transporting various items of equipment.

It was therefore important for the vehicles to be stable and horizontal so that precision work could be carried out inside the technical bodies. For this the chassis was fitted with three sets of stabilizers, one at the front, one at the rear, and the third just behind the cab, but this one was often removed as it was not thought to be of much use.

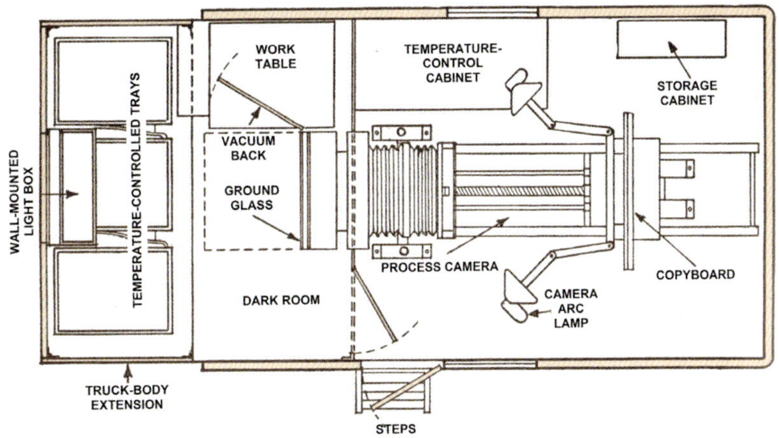

Top left: Each object selected for photographing was positioned on a fixed vertical support; with the bellows extended, the more or less distant setting gives a result as close as possible to what was wanted. This precision work was only possible when the vehicle was not moving. (U.S. Army Air Forces)

Top right: Diagram of how the inside of a Camera Section truck was set out. The bellows section takes up most of the space available in the technical body. (Source TM 5-245)

Above: The impressive size of the bellows camera installed in the Camera Section truck is quite clear here. While Pvt Howard D. Rothman and T/4 Thomas L. Woolford are setting the lenses, T/5 Andrew McDonald at the back of the vehicle is finishing off developing the latest impressed plate. (U.S. Army Air Forces)

In the case of the Diamond Ts, the versions were:

- Camera Section trucks with 24-inch/30-inch cameras. It was in these trucks that the photos were taken from which the maps were made by and for the Army; but it was also with this equipment that reproducing existing documents or images was possible by re-photographing them. Once taken, the photograph was developed directly in the rear part of the vehicle and sent to the Plate Process Section (equipped with GMC trucks) which engraved the images on metal plates before sending them to the printing presses.
- Press Section trucks with two different interior fittings, either 20-inch/22½-inch or 22-inch/29-inch presses. This was the final stage of the impressions before they were distributed to those concerned.

Using the Diamond T rather than the GMC was not especially dictated by the work surfaces because, without the rear extension, there was only a difference of 9½ feet^2 on the ground (90 feet^2 for the GMC as against 99½ feet^2 for the Diamond T). The choice was made because of the robustness of the truck, as in this configuration the GMC could in theory only carry 4,750 lb whereas the Diamond T still using this configuration of technical body could carry 6,800 lb, over a ton more which made all the difference when it came to heavy printing equipment.

Right: Diagram of how the inside of a Press Section truck was set out; here again the imposing printing press takes up most of the space available. (Source TM 5-245)

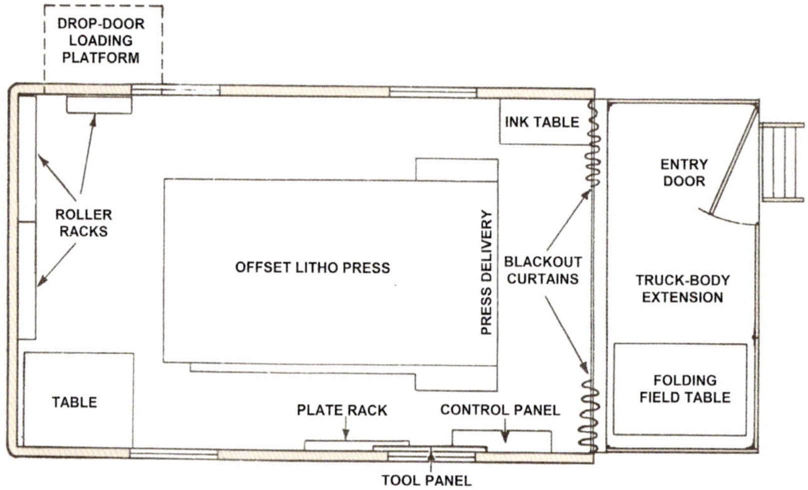

Below right: Somewhere in Germany on a detour road built by the Engineers, the 665th Engineer Topographic Battalion is moving in a long convoy. The first vehicle is a Press Section truck mounted on a Diamond T chassis, followed by a Dodge WC-52, and two smaller-sized map reproduction trucks, on GMC CCKW chassis. (Private Collection)

Below: It was important for the truck to be stable and horizontal both widthwise and lengthwise so the work could be done in optimal conditions. As the stabilizing jacks could only be extended a certain distance, piles of blocks were often used to ensure that stabilization was perfect. (Private Collection)

Right: With its registration number USA-4450960, this Diamond T 968A has been identified as a bare, long-wheelbase chassis from a series of 126 vehicles that were part of contract no. W-398-QM-W-662. (Private Collection)

Below: This map reproduction truck belongs to the 949th Engineer Topographic Battalion of the Third Air Force. After it had been set up in a horizontal and stable position, the electricity needed for it to work properly was supplied by the generator in the background. (Private Collection)

Asphalt Tank 800-Gallon, Truck-Mounted

According to the definition in the TM 5-1148 technical manual, the vehicle's designation was Asphalt Tank 800-Gallon, Truck-Mounted, Rosco Model RMU, or in normal English, the Rosco Model RMU, 800-gallon truck-mounted asphalt tank.

Mounted on a 151-inch wheelbase Diamond T 968A truck, the technical part of the vehicle comprised an insulated tank, the machinery required for keeping the asphalt at a working temperature, and what was necessary for pouring it where it was needed. Some 177 examples were ordered for the Corps of Engineers.

It was Rosco of Minneapolis that was given the job of supplying and installing its Model RMU equipment on the Diamond T chassis. This mainly comprised a platform taking an 800-gallon electrically welded elliptical metal tank, a Gorman-Rupp centrifugal pump, and all the piping needed for transferring the liquids. Working independently using a 1,506-cc (91.9-cubic inch) Wisconsin VF-41 gasoline engine, rated at 20.5 hp at 2,200 rpm, the RMU model had a manual spray lance linked up to the truck with soft piping.

Top and above: The silhouette of the 800-gallon, truck-mounted asphalt tank appears identical to the 1,000-gallon truck-mounted water distributor as the bases were so similar. To be able to produce such a compact vehicle, the tank was shorter and it therefore carried less so that it could house the pump equipment and the engine at the rear. Access to the platform was no longer by the side, hence the disappearance of the steps. (Source TM 5-1148)

Left: The 800-gallon, truck-mounted asphalt tank was mainly designed to carry out precision work, like filling in joints between slabs or laying tarred sheets for waterproofing. It was also used to supply teams laying runways using PBS (Prefabricated Bituminous Surfacing) and its long, coated strips. The undercoat was thus poured directly onto the ground with the help of the portable lance. (Source TM 5-1148)

Bituminous Tank 800-Gallon, Truck-Mounted

The TM 5-11.4 technical manual indexes this vehicle as the Bituminous Tank, Truck-Mounted, 800-Gallon, Etnyre Model MX-D6, or in normal parlance, the Etnyre Model MX-D6, 800-gallon, truck-mounted bituminous tank. Mounted on the base of a 151-inch wheelbase Diamond T 968A truck, the technical part of the vehicle comprised an insulated tank, machinery for keeping the asphalt at the working temperature and a large, folding spray boom. Some 285 examples were delivered to the Engineers.

Etnyre was given the task of supplying and fitting its Model MX-D6 equipment onto the Diamond T chassis. This consisted mainly of a platform taking an 800-gallon electrically welded elliptical metal tank, a centrifugal pump, and all the piping needed for transferring the liquids. It worked independently using a 1,666.86-cc (101.7-cubic inch) LeRoi D-140 gasoline engine, rated at 26 hp at 2,100 rpm.

Above and right: What characterized these trucks was the volume of the machinery. To house the LeRoi engine, the designers had to position it lengthwise and give it a large overhang at the rear. This position meant the chassis had to be lengthened and the towing gear disposed of, replaced with two simple hooks. (Source TM 5-1134)

Below: Somewhere in India, on the 1333rd U.S. Army Air Forces base of the Air Transport Command: maintaining the main runway is just about completed. To stabilize the repairs and the gravelling, an 800-gallon, truck-mounted bituminous tank has extended its spraying booms, spreading its liquid bitumen. In this configuration, the swathe is close to 26 feet wide. (U.S. Army Air Forces ref. 74881 -A.C.)

Other Special Trucks

The needs of the different services meant that some very specific vehicles were created. As these were hardly ever cataloged, they are almost impossible to find in the various delivery and order registers. For at least one of them, it was not even a matter of being adapted by a sub-contractor; only a conversion kit is mentioned. The three most notable creations were mounted on the 172-inch-wheelbase, long-chassis Diamond T 968A truck.

Oil Field Body Truck or Flatbed Truck

These were transport vehicles used for moving heavy and cumbersome equipment like pumps, valves, and other engines used by the Engineer pipeline companies when setting up networks for channeling fuel supplies over long distances. To create the truck initially meant installing a kit called the pipe-line equipment set supplied by the company Roehik. The kit included the loading platform, a cab protector, a removable lifting hoist, a 20,000-lb power winch installed transversally behind the cab, a PTO to be fitted to the truck, plus accessories and work tackle.

Rotary Drill Truck-Mounted

These truck-mounted rotary drills were drilling derricks used by the Engineer water company for drilling wells down to the water table to ensure potable water supplies where lakes and rivers were not accessible. They were able to drill with 5-inch-diameter trepans, down to a depth of 1,000 feet, depending on the hardness of the ground. All the machinery was independent of the truck. Power was obtained from a 217-hp Buda engine which drove all the hydraulic drilling equipment, coupled to a Gardner-Denver aspiration pump. Operations were carried out from the truck to which was attached a foldable derrick.

Tractor Trucks

Tractor trucks were intended for transporting long objects of which one half of their mass rested on a pivoting pedestal and the other half on a trailer with extendable shaft, of the pole-hauling type, with a single or double axle. This assembly was a specialty of the Eidel Manufacturing Co., and consisted mainly of a central bolster, a double-guide roller installed on the end of the chassis traverses, and an imposing cab protector.

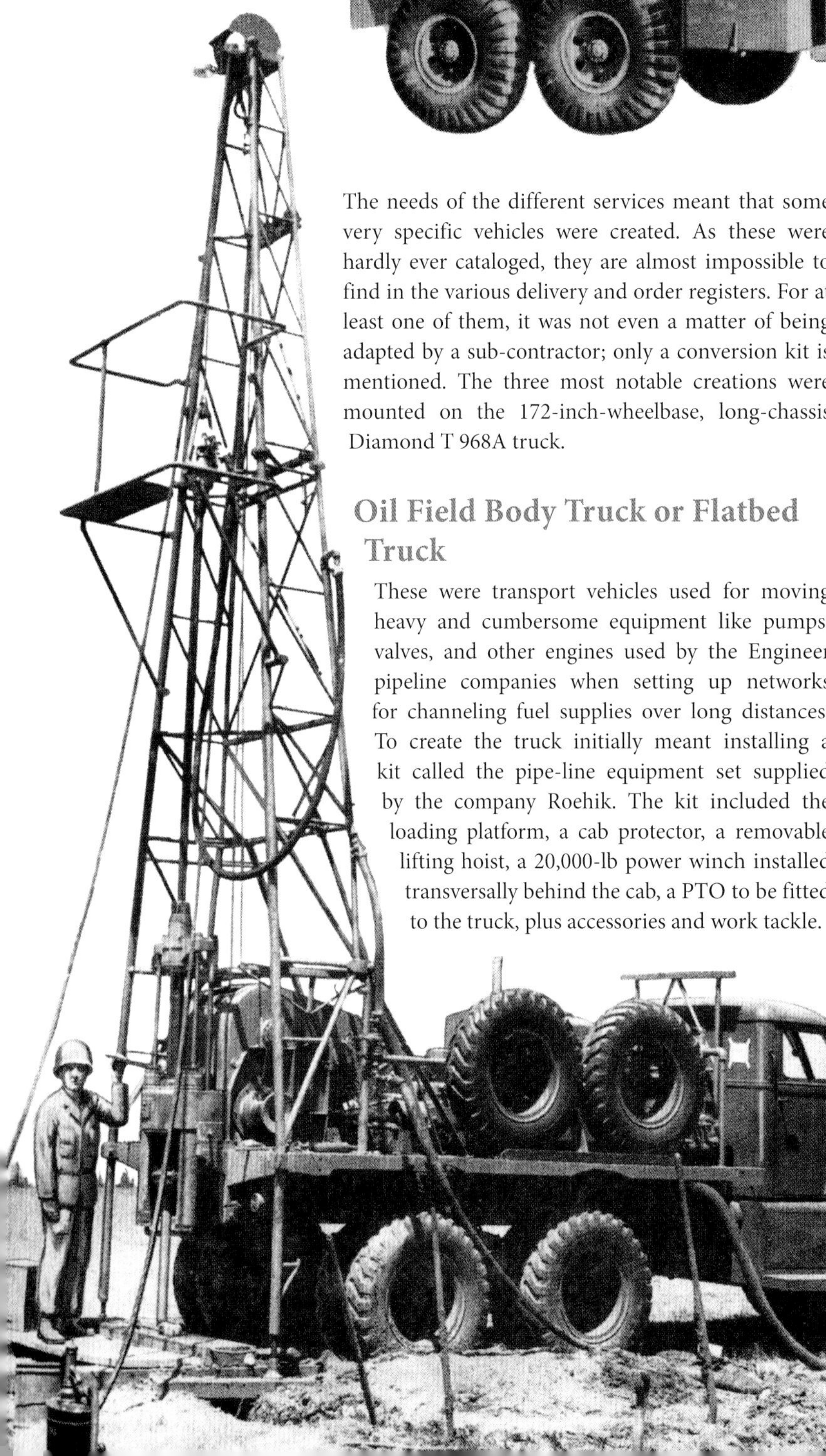

Above: This simplified example of an oil field body truck does not have a lifting hoist. Working in areas with no infrastructure, these trucks had to be completely autonomous, hence the rear winch and the lifting gantry. (Source TM 9-2800)

Left: Like the majority of vehicles designed on the Diamond T bare chassis, only a few rotary drill trucks were built. Fortunately, the technical manuals of the Corps of Engineers means they are documented. (Source TM 5-297)

Left: Sun Valley on Guadalcanal, June 10, 1944, the 798th Engineer Forestry Company in action with one of its Diamond T tractor trucks. Loaded with two enormous logs, the driver is heading for the field sawmill. The ensemble comprises a twin-wheeled double-axle pole-hauling trailer. (U.S. Army Signal Corps)

Below left: April 1945, rebuilding the Rhine crossing structures. As the bridges had been destroyed, the Engineers had the important task of making Germany accessible as directly and as fast as possible, including by train. This Diamond T tractor truck is transporting entire sections of rail track spans which the cranes will simply unload and lay. (U.S. Army Signal Corps)

Below: With its registration no. USA-4605195, this example was part of a series of 42 vehicles diverted from their original cargo job and delivered in the bare chassis form. This truck from the Engineer battalion of the 7th Infantry Division has been fitted with a small fifth wheel, which has converted it to a tractor truck. (Private Collection)

11 Special Services

All throughout the conflict, many vehicles of all makes were modified and adapted to the service and the operational requirements of their users.

In the case of the Diamond T, the rear part of the trucks was well and truly rebuilt. It was no longer a question of DIY work on the spot but real modifications carried out at the highest levels of the maintenance chain.

There was no doubt that the services of the Quartermaster Corps or the Ordnance Department did as much as they could to equip units with the best mechanical equipment available. It was a question of supplying vehicles with the most extensive capabilities, whilst at the same time covering as widely as possible the specific needs of the different components of the U.S. Army. Nonetheless, despite all the diligence, there were certain circumstances that were not taken into account by those in the planning departments.

Special Service, Shop Truck

The 4-ton, 6x6 truck range readily lent itself to large-scale modifications. A number of cargo trucks were fitted with structures that converted them into large workshop vehicles. Indeed, the standard-issue vehicles, like the CCKW-353 with an ordnance maintenance or motorized shop technical body, or the Ford 29W shop engineer truck, were not always up to the tasks required of them.

Opposite: Marianas, late 1944, this B-29 Superfortress *Pacific Queen* of the 500th Bomb Group of 21st Bomber Command is being serviced after five sorties over Japan. Men from a mobile repair unit of the Air Force Service Group have converted a Diamond T 968A into a mobile workshop by building a rigid structure and installing a lifting jib using the truck's winch. (U.S. Army Air Forces ref. 56849 -A.C.)

Maintenance, repairs, salvages, and recoveries were the daily lot of those units tasked with keeping the air fleet operational. What most of these conversions in the field had in common was the use of the telescopic boom for lifting operations. With its 5-ton capacity, it was designed to function using the winch cable for operations requiring a lot of power, though a manual hoist was preferable for the finicky jobs because it was more precise. (U.S. Army Air Forces ref. 64826 -A.C.)

Left: Various rigid shapes were mounted on the cargo bodies, from the simplest to the more complex. Note the corbeled part above the cab to increase the work and storage space. Quite often, however, it was just rigid side panels surmounted by the standard tarpaulin and thereby heightened that gave more standing room. (U.S. Army Air Forces ref. 58274-A.C.)

Special Service, Platform Truck

In the combat zones where the Transportation Corps' roadgoing units were not as yet present, few trucks were able to carry the cumbersome freight unloaded from the boats.

The AFKWX-353 and the Ford GBT combination stake and platform trucks were too small, so once again it was the Diamond Ts which were used. The cargo trucks fitted with wooden bodies were modified for operational needs, the body side panels, the tailgate, and the side rails being removed to leave a loading platform without any obstacles.

Right: There was nothing risky about modifying the wooden cargo body. Here, no fewer than three Diamond T 968/968As have been converted in this way. As soon as the trucks and trailers are loaded, they will make for a motor base where they will be unloaded at the end of a vehicle reassembly line. This one is transporting crated Jeeps. So as not to handicap the trucks, the side of the crate nearest the cab has been left in place, enabling the two spare-wheel supports to be retained. (U.S. Army SC-377501)

Below: The loading capacity of the Diamond T 968/968As enabled them to carry sizable loads, though only if the cargo body sides had been removed, which was only possible if the cargo bodies were made of wood. Here, in a New Caledonian port, September 10, 1943, the crates contain differentials for two GMC CCKW-353s without winches. The upper one contains Banjo axle sets from GMC, the lower one Split axle sets from Timken, Detroit, as stenciled on the sides of the packing crates. (U.S. Army SC-377502)

Above: Military cartage comprised a number of stake and platform trailers, with removable sides, so there was no need to modify them to convert them into bare platforms. As a pair, this configuration is more effective and easier to use than the one consisting of a 4x4 tractor and a semi-trailer. (U.S. Army SC-377503)

Right: Registration no. 461616 for this former Diamond T 968A cargo truck, converted to a 950-gallon gasoline tank truck. The tank's relatively small capacity caused the tank to be lower than the cab, with a single filler opening and access on the top. In this form, the vehicle was 268 inches long, 96 inches wide, and 98 inches high. Its empty weight was 17,600 lb, its payload was 5,700 lb for a total mass of 22,300 lb. (U.S. Army Signal Corps)

Special Service, Gasoline Tank

Although the cargo body conversions were simple enough, this was not the case with the tank trucks. Engineer units were fuel-thirsty and tractors towing semi-trailer tanks struggled to keep up with the Engineers' technical vehicles in the vast construction sites en route to Japan. In many cases, the CCKW-353 Tank, Gasoline 750 Gallons (or CCKW-353, 750-gallon gasoline tank truck, in normal English) in service was too small to properly satisfy supply demand, so Diamond T trucks were modified into tank trucks and appropriate trailers built.

Be they the cargo body or the bare chassis versions, two types of tanks were installed on the Diamond T 968/968As: a small 950-gallon tank and a large 1,350-gallon tank. Both were made of welded metal plate, were oval and comprised one single compartment. Three types of homemade

The 1,350-gallon gasoline tank version is more imposing, with its tank sticking up above the level of the truck cab roof, and its two upper access panels. Registration no. 461206 for this former 968A cargo truck. In this form, the vehicle was 268 inches long, 96 inches wide, and 104 inches high. Its empty weight was 18,100 lb, its payload was 8,100 lb for a total mass of 26,200 lb. The location of the spare wheel was common to both vehicles, as well as the total absence of mudguards and mud flaps. (U.S. Army Signal Corps)

The 782nd Engineer Petroleum Distribution Company, May 2, 1945 near Manila, Luzon, Philippines. A 1,350-gallon Diamond T gasoline tank truck is filling its tank via a distribution gantry. To make operations easier, lateral gangways have been fitted onto the truck. (U.S. Army Signal Corps)

Registration no. 461558 for this Diamond T 968A cargo converted to a 950-gallon gasoline tank truck. The tank capacity is identifiable by the tank's height behind the cab and the single filler opening. It is once again the registration number that enables the vehicle to be identified and its overall administrative characteristics to be defined. The number 461558 refers to a series of 231 identical trucks included in order no. W-398-QM-10140 placed in 1941 by the Quartermaster Corps. In this order, 637 vehicles of this type were recorded, 605 of which were taken on charge in 1941, the others in 1942. (U.S. Army Signal Corps)

trailers were hitched up to these tank-trucks with capacities of 600, 1,800, and 2,350 gallons; all three were designed in the same way as those mounted on the modified trucks. Being homemade, these trucks and trailers had no way of pumping the liquids back as they only worked by gravity.

Trailer, 4-Wheel, Gasoline Tank, 600 Gallons

The first trailer in the order of capacity was 144 inches long, 76 inches wide, and 72 inches high; its empty weight was 5,200 lb, its payload 3,600 lb for a total mass of 8,800 lb. (U.S. Army Signal Corps)

Trailer, 4-Wheel, Gasoline Tank, 1,800 Gallons

The second trailer in the order of capacity was 216 inches long, 96 inches wide, and 72 inches high; its empty weight was 8,100 lb, its payload 10,800 lb for a total mass of 18,900 lb. (U.S. Army Signal Corps)

Trailer, 4-Wheel, Gasoline Tank, 2,350 Gallons

The third trailer in the order of capacity was 204 inches long, 96 inches wide, and 87 inches high; its empty weight was 8,650 lb, its payload 14,100 lb for a total mass of 22,750 lb. (U.S. Army Signal Corps)

Special Service, Water Tank

This other variation based on a Diamond T 968/968A truck was a multi-task design, using a water tank containing 1,350 gallons. The truck could be used as a simple water transport, an auxiliary supply unit for teams using a fire truck, or as a sprinkler truck for watering roads, with its 8 feet 6 inches-wide built-on spraying boom. It was entirely self-sufficient, with a four-cylinder gasoline engine, associated to a centrifugal pump which functioned both for filling the vat and for sprinkling operations or various supply operations.

Above: Registration no. USA-486571 for this former Diamond T 9658A cargo truck converted to a 1,350-gallon sprinkler tank and auxiliary fire truck. In this configuration, the vehicle was 286 inches long, 96 inches wide, and 92 inches high. It weighed 20,100 lb empty, with a payload of 4,903 lb, for a total mass of 30,900 lb. (U.S. Army Signal Corps)

Right: Protruding over the end, the imposing machinery was set out on a work shelf where all the piping for loading and unloading, together with the connection for linking it to a fire truck, was brought together. In extreme cases, the truck could itself be used as a fire engine: it carried about 40 feet of soft fire hoses and a nozzle for controlling the water jet. (U.S. Army Signal Corps)

12 Halftracks

It may seem strange to find halftracks among a truck builder's product range. It was indeed those industries specializing in building heavy tonnage trucks that shared the production of some 55,500 halftracks ordered by the U.S. Army.

Although one associates names such as the White Motor Co., Autocar Co., or International Harvester Co. with producing halftracks, the Diamond T Motor Car Co. does not immediately spring to mind. The company went on to produce some 22% of the total number of these vehicles, with 12,111 units put into service in four models: 7,410 M3 personnel carriers, 3,413 M3A1 personnel carriers, 963 T-48 57-mm gun motor carriages, and 325 T19 105-mm howitzer carriages.

Right and below: Be they Whites, Autocars, or Diamond Ts, all the halftracks made by these three builders used the same mechanics. The basic components came from the same suppliers, giving rational optimization, the main benefit of which was in servicing the fleet of halftracks, no matter who the builder. (U.S. Army SC-120021 & 120022)

Disregarding the International Harvester-built vehicles, the halftracks produced by the other three companies were built along identical lines with almost 100% of their components being common to all three. Only a few details like the numbering of the chassis, for instance, distinguished a White halftrack from an Autocar or a Diamond T.

DIAMOND T MOTOR CAR CO. HALFTRACK PRODUCTION				
Quantities	Orders	Registration No.	Series No.	Comments
Personnel Carrier M3				
2,000	W-741-ORD-6289	W-401782 to W-403781	1904 to 3903	All with crossing roller
610	W-271-ORD-600	W-4027649 to W-4028258	4304 to 4913	All with crossing roller
1	W-271-ORD-853	W-4029242	5523	With crossing roller
1,000	W-271-ORD-964	W-4043329 to W-4044328	7072 to 8071	All with crossing roller
600	W-271-ORD-965	W-4045909 to W-4046508	6472 to 7071	All with crossing roller
238	W-271-ORD-1023	W-40111266 to 40111503	8072 to 8309	179 with winch and 59 with crossing roller
800	W-271-ORD-1023	W-40102634 to 40103433	8310 to 9109	600 with winch and 200 with crossing roller
982	W-271-ORD-1385	W-4028260 to W-4029241	10275 to 11256	460 with winch and 422 with crossing roller
1,000	W-271-ORD-1967	W-4054460 to W-4055459	22831 to 23830	750 with winch and 250 with crossing roller
179	W-271-ORD-2642	W-40104254 to W-40104432	30121 to 30299	135 with winch and 44 with crossing roller
Or a total of 7,410 M3 personnel carriers built by the Diamond T Motor Car Co. for the U.S. Army. 2,124 built with a winch and 5,286 built with a crossing roller. 61 examples destroyed, rebuilt as M3 personnel carriers. 2,289 examples modified as M3A1 personnel carriers: 844 by Wylie Inc. and 1,445 by Bowen & McLaughlin. 1,164 units delivered in the context of the Lend-Lease were added to the production, giving a total production of 8,573 M3A1 personnel carriers. 1,087 were taken on charge in 1941, 3,905 in 1942, and 3,581 in 1943.				
Personnel Carrier M3A1				
3,110	W-271-ORD-2432	W-4062092 to W-4065201	23831 to 26940	2,333 with winch and 777 with crossing roller
273	W-271-ORD-2727	W-40104705 to W-40104705	30300 to 30572	205 with winch and 68 with crossing roller
30	W-271-ORD-2726	W-40111227 to W-40111256	30848 to 30877	All with winch
Or a total of 3,413 M3A1 personnel carriers built by the Diamond T Motor Car Co. for the U.S. Army. 2,568 built with a winch and 845 built with a crossing roller. 1,737 were taken on charge in 1943 and 1,676 in 1944.				
Gun Motor Carriage T-48 (57mm)				
1	Prototype	None	None	Aberdeen Proving Ground
681	W-271-ORD-1023	W-4020934 to W-4021614	None	
281*	W-271-ORD-1023	None	None	All modified to M3A1 Personnel Carriers
Or a total of 963 T-48 57-mm gun motor carriages. 50 delivered in December 1942 and 912 in 1943 (174 in January, 250 in February, 200 in March, 250 in April, and 38 in May). 50 intended for England but in the end only 30 delivered (to India). 651 to Russia. * The 281 were modified at Chester Tank Depot in 1944 and were given the serial numbers 40241 to 40521.				
Howitzer Motor Carriage T19 (105 mm)				
1	–	–	1	Aberdeen Proving Ground
324*	W-741-ORD-6289	W-403377 to W-403698	2 to 323	180 modified to M3A1 personnel carriers in 1945
Or a total of 325 T19 105-mm howitzer motor carriages. * 324 in 1942 (38 in February, 136 in March, 149 in April).				

Original organization for this bare front, with headlamps behind small grilles and marker lights with bluish lenses for forward blackout lighting. (U.S. Army Signal Corps)

General Mechanics

It was the 160 AX-type engine by the White Motor Co that was chosen to power the vehicles of the three main builders. It was a 6,327-cc (386-cubic inch), six-cylinder, water-cooled gasoline engine rated at 147 bhp at 3,000 rpm. It was coupled to a single plate, dry disc clutch, and a Spicer Model 3641 gearbox with four forward and one reverse gears, and a two-speed transfer box used also to engage the front differential if needed. Note that at the start of production, engaging the low ratio of the transfer box could be done without engaging the front differential. The subsequent incorporation of an interlock mechanism theoretically prevented this from happening. The mechanical chain was completed by Timken-Detroit Model F35-HX-1 Split-type differentials at the front and Model 56410-

Here a series of chassis for halftracks with winches arrive by train directly in the assembly buildings. (Diamond T Co.)

Assembling and preparing the chassis. The workers position the main elements for installing the mechanical parts. Everything was done by hand, with no sophisticated installations or complex assembly lines such as at Ford. It was almost the work of craftsmen. (Diamond T Co.)

BX-67 Banjo-type for driving the tracks, the latter being located in the middle of the chassis.

Quite obviously, the main characteristic of the halftrack, hence the name, was the tracked running gear at the rear. Apart from the intermediary differential, there was also a tension idler wheel. With time and the weaknesses encountered, in November 1942, its retaining frame was modified in order to, among other things, incorporate a recovery tether for the side tension forces and a longitudinal front spring. With overall a smaller diameter and a greater length to start with, this spring was then modified to become thicker but shorter.

On both sides the vehicle rested on four sets of two rollers with rubber stripping. Linked in pairs, these sets enabled the difference in the terrain to be absorbed, while at the same time guiding the teeth of the tracks. On either side of the chassis, an intermediary running gear support received a double-track retention caster with the suspension elements

The depot where the transmissions to be installed on the chassis were stocked. (Diamond T Co.)

As soon as the chassis received the differentials and track rollers for the rear running gear, they were advanced in two long lines inside the assembly building. On each side, stocks of sub-assemblies make up well defined assembly points. (Diamond T Co.)

located inside it. Side cages, closed in on the early productions, were allocated two oblong vents enabling them to be unblocked and cleaned.

Ground contact was through two 8.25x20 standard 10-ply (with an inner tube) or combat-type 12-ply (puncture-proof) tires and rubber 12-inch-wide tracks with 58 links from the B. F. Goodrich Co. which had a bearing capacity along the ground of 46¾ inches.

Two models of tracks followed each other; although they both had external side protective blocks that served to prevent chains sliding, early production was characterized by bigger blocks in which a gorge was drawn to receive the metal links (track grousers) in order to increase the traction on soft terrain.

The relatively high degree of comfort for a halftrack was ensured on the front differential by double-action

Bit by bit, the vehicles took shape; in the foreground is a chassis with its reinforced structure, to be used as the base for the gun carriage which will be fitted with the 57-mm gun of the T-48 gun motor carriage. (Diamond T Co.)

In the bodywork workshop, the various elements are assembled on the base which will cover the rear part of the chassis—the start of assembling the combat compartments. (Diamond T Co.)

hydraulic shock absorbers with adjustable resistance, and by sets of 11 semi-elliptical leaves. On the rear, on each side, a pair of helical springs was incorporated into the inside of the intermediary supports of the running gear. This overall configuration, together with a 60-gallon fuel capacity split between two tanks located in the rear part of the armored body, gave the halftracks a range of 200 miles or an average consumption of 3.33 miles per gallon.

Although the initial projects were totally in phase with the scout-car design and the crossing roller on the front fender, the value of fitting the halftracks, or at least some of them, with a winch became obvious. This was installed on a support as a forward extension of the chassis, and was operated through a Brown-Lipe Model 001904 PTO fitted on the left of the gearbox and transfer box units. The winch was from Tulsa, an 18G-type with a pulling power of 10,000 lb.

The engineers paid particular attention to the technical specifications of the vehicle, no matter what the configuration, such as its mass and speed. The result was a hydraulic braking system comprising a master

Installing the rear bodywork, assembled with a work frame which made handling easier and enabled the operation to be done in one go. (Diamond T Co.)

cylinder commanded by a simple power-assisted pedal coupled to a brake power cylinder located on the outside of the left longeron of the chassis. From this master cylinder, two pipes fed each of the two differentials, to each drum and its slave cylinder.

With time, as with other vehicles in the U.S. Army, replacing the cylinder with the sophisticated Hydrovac from Bendix became commonplace on the assembly lines. The parking brake, also considered as the emergency and breakdown brake, was located at the exit of the auxiliary gearbox and controlled directly by a lever in the driving cab. Originally intended for multi-purpose roles, the halftrack was supplied the components needed to tow trailers fitted with electric brakes.

The halftrack's electrical installation was designed around a 12-volt system (negative earth), using a Willard 240-amp/h battery situated in an external compartment under the front right-hand door. The vehicle's front lighting was made up of two large independent headlights with sealed beams, fitted to the wings and protected by metal grilles. There were also two smaller marker lights with bluish lenses.

The rear lighting comprised completely removable units equipped with bulbs, all the lights being controlled from the dashboard by a pull switch. The rear light bulbs were replaced by watertight, non-removable blocks and the marker lights by blackout fender lights which remained standard until the end of production.

During 1942, all American vehicles had to be fitted with blackout drive lights, this novelty being used to modify the forward lighting. Considered justifiably as a combat vehicle, the halftrack had to be able to maneuver without lighting, like the M8 armored car for instance, and removing the headlights so that the vehicle was not lit up by accident was recommended.

DIAMOND T HALFTRACK TECHNICAL SPECIFICATIONS

	Personnel Carrier M3	Personnel Carrier M3A1	Gun Motor Carriage T-48	Howitzer Motor Carriage T19
No. of examples built	7,410	3,413	3,413	325
Length [1]	242.63 in	242.63 in	242.63 in	242.63 in
Width [2]	77.25 in	77.25 in	77.25 in	77.25 in
Height [3]	89 in	106 in	89 in	89 in
Wheelbase	135.5 in	135.5 in	135.5 in	135 in
Crew	13 men	13 men	5 men	6 men
Weight [4]	16,514.83 lb	17,015.28 lb	19,817.36 lb	17,414.32 lb
Payload	3,503.15 lb	3,503.15 lb	2,502.25 lb	2,601.46 lb
Angle of attack [5]	37°	37°	37°	37°
Angle of exit	35°	35°	35°	35°
Max. slope	60°	60°	60°	60°
Vertical obstacle	12 in	12 in	12 in	12 in
Fording capability	32 in	32 in	32 in	32 in
Front armor	0.25 in	0.25 in	0.25 in	0.25 in
Rear armor	0.25 in	0.25 in	0.25 in	0.25 in
Side armor	0.25 in	0.25 in	0.25 in	0.25 in
Bonnet armor	0.25 in	0.25 in	0.25 in	0.25 in
Windshield armor	0.50 in	0.50 in	0.50 in	0.50 in
Main weapon	1 x .30-cal MG	1 x .50-cal MG	1 x 57-mm cannon	1 x 105-mm cannon
Secondary weapon	–	1 x .30-cal MG	–	1 x .50-cal MG
.30-cal ammunition	4,000 units	7,750 units	–	–
.50-cal ammunition	–	700 units	–	300 units
57-mm shells	–	–	99 units	–
105-mm shells	–	–	–	8 units

1. When a winch was installed instead of the crossing roller, the length increased by 6.85 inches.
2. When mine-carrying side racks were installed, the width increased by 10.25 inches.
3. The heights do not take into account the fitting of the main weapons.
4. The difference in weight with a winch fitted was 423,77 lb.
5. When a winch was fitted the angle of attack decreased by 3°.

As soon as they were completed and tested, the new halftracks were carefully lined up, ready for delivery to the Army. (Diamond T Co.)

The blackout fender lights formed a unit with the headlights and were mounted on rods which were lodged in special housings on either side of the radiator grille. When not in use, they were placed in supports installed in the combat compartment and were replaced by blackout drive and blackout fender light units.

It is not possible to list here all the modifications that affected the overall evolution of the halftrack; they were so numerous and some more anecdotal than anything else. Note the changes made to the engine cooling system, for example, by removing the cab heating system fitted into the circuit, the various variations to the suspension, wheels, rims, running gear, mountings for the crossing roller, accessories to the engine, and elements on the dashboard.

The second model of road lighting for halftracks. For blackout use, the second lights replaced the first which were fitted on spikes. (U.S. Army Signal Corps)

The Overall Shape

The halftrack grew directly from the M3A1 scout car, from which it borrowed the front and the style of the combat compartment. All its armor was made from ¼-inch-thick laminated and tempered steel, except for the windshield's protective mask which was ½ an inch thick. Simply intended to protect against small-arms fire, the peripheral armor was absolutely vertical; the radiator protection had a 25° slope, the windshield 26°, and the hood 83°. To facilitate production and reduce costs, all these elements were assembled bolted together. Three parts of the halftrack carapace were removable: the windshield mask which was held horizontal by three small struts when not in use, the door shutters, and the radiator protection. Made up of four horizontal slats, the latter pivoted using a lever operated from inside the driver's post by the co-driver. Five positions enabled it to shut or open the strips, with three intermediary positions.

M3 Personnel Carrier

The personnel carrier halftracks built by the Diamond T Motor Car Co. were just as numerous as those built by Autocar or White and were all mixed up when delivered to the units.

Above: Fort Benning, February 1942, an M3 personnel carrier in the 2nd Armored Division. Its registration no. USA-W-401855 indicates it was part of order W-741-ORD-6289, or the first contract placed for vehicles of this type with Diamond T. (U.S. Army SC-132159)

Left: Carpark at Camp Shelby, August 1941. USA-W-401891, USA-W-401889, and USA-W-401873 for these three Diamond T M3 personnel carriers from order no. W-741-ORD-6289. Judging by the succession of numbers, one can assume that these vehicles were delivered as entire lots. (U.S. Army SC-122713)

Large-scale maneuvers in the Californian desert in 1942. An M3 Diamond T is in difficulty at the bottom of a sandy gully. Registration no. USA-W-402824, from contract no. W-741-ORD-6289, which was the biggest grouped order, with 2,000 vehicles. (U.S. Army SC-143193)

Early Production

The personnel carriers or squad carriers, depending on the reference documents, were ultimately the only armored versions of the troop transport trucks, like the GMC CCKW for example. Intended, among other things, for transporting armored division infantry, they were designed to carry 13 men including the driver. There were two rows of cushions, each for five men, installed lengthwise in the combat compartment with three seats in the diver's cab. Behind these three seats were two fuel tanks as well as two storage bays also used as racks for personal weapons.

A water-cooled, 4,000-round .30-cal. M 1917 A1 machine gun on an M25 pedestal mount was installed for vehicle defense. Also among the onboard armament was a .45-cal. Thomson machine pistol with 540 rounds and 20 to 22 grenades. The M3 had storage space in the floor as well as under the cushions at the rear.

The M3 was the perfect small tractor for smaller-caliber ordnance, like this 2-inch antiaircraft gun at Camp Young, September 17, 1942. This Diamond T example was part of contract no. W-271-ORD-964 with registration no. USA-W-4042793. (U.S. Army SC-144920)

Mid-production

The M3 personnel carriers from mid-production were not too different from the preceding versions. They simply followed the range's technological evolution. The machine gun was now a .30-cal. air-cooled M1919 A4. The idler wheel tension system was given the first then the second spring tension mechanism. Finally, new headlights, interchangeable with the blackout drive lamps, were installed, which necessitated minor modifications made inside the combat post for their storage.

Late Production

The end of production brought together all the modifications leading to the final version of the model, including positioning racks on the sides for carrying 24 antitank mines.

Right: Apart from the crossing roller on the front, this example is the definitive version of the M3 halftrack with side racks for carrying mines, and lighting consisting of either mounts for the road lamps or the blackout lights. With all its protective shutters shut, this Diamond T M3 is from order no. W-ORD-1023 with registration no. USA-40103375. (U.S. Army Signal Corps)

Right and opposite top: The Desert Training Center, August 1942. M3 Diamond T personnel carrier with registration no. USA-W-4027980 which links it to contract W-271-ORD-600 and the 610 examples ordered. Although the SCR-299 radio was meant to be installed as a priority in the Chevrolet 1½-ton, 4x4 panel trucks under the Signal Corps' K-51 designation, the Armored Board tried to get its armored vehicles fitted with it. The M3 had adequate internal capacity for housing all the equipment; heightening the tarpaulin hoops gave the personnel standing room, and the generator in the K-52 trailer supplied the electricity. This 1-ton trailer is the early model with an inflatable tire on its jockey wheel. (U.S. Army SC-144992 and 144993)

General Usage

Apart from its simple role of armored transport, the M3 personnel carrier was then brought out with a host of uses for the armored divisions and accompanying units. It was the uncluttered interior and the access from the rear that made it preferable to its predecessor, the M2, so much so that it took on the task of ammunition carrier, a job it was not intended for. But be they the infantry units, the Signal Corps, the Corps of Engineers or even the Medical Department, the protection the M3 personnel carrier provided against small-arms fire was much appreciated by the troops.

The Diamond T Motor Co. supplied the Army with 7,410 examples of this version of the halftrack, of which 5,186 were built with a crossing roller at the front, and 2,124 with a standard winch. In the upgrade program, 2,289 of these 7,410 M3s were converted to M3A1s. As part of the Lend-Lease program, the 1,164 units supplied to Allied nations should be added.

Who was better placed to pay tribute to the Diamond T halftrack production than General George Patton? Coming from order W-741-ORD-6289 with registration number USA-W-402408, this M3 is the personification of this extraordinary character. Armored roof, side protections on the rear running gear, complex radio installation, and pennants for the commander of I Armored Corps made it a rather indiscreet command vehicle. (U.S. Army SC-144994)

M3A1 Personnel Carrier

Logically, the M3s were developed in the same way as the M2s and were also fitted with the M-49 ring mount above the co-driver's seat which converted it to an M3A1. As all the technical steps had been taken for the M2A1, there were no specific trials before the M3A1 was built—this was one of the advantages of standardization—and no interior refitting needed to be done. The vehicle's armament still comprised a single .30-cal. machine gun set up on three fixed mounts on each side of the combat post.

When the 12.7-mm gun arrived, fixation points had to be fitted on the outside of the rear door for storing the tripod. The ammunition issued comprised 700 .50-cal. rounds, 7,750 .30-cal. rounds, 540 machine pistol .45 rounds, 22 grenades, and 24 antitank mines.

Classifying the M3A1s as standard vehicles in April 1943 meant that the M3s automatically went into the Substitute Standard Vehicle category, delivered when the M3A1 was not available. Six months passed between this order in April and the realities

Left: The landings on the Normandy beaches. The 17th Armored Engineer Battalion of the 2nd Armored Division borrowed a ramp for getting off Omaha Beach. USA-W-4062301 for this M3A1 Diamond T personnel carrier from contract no. W-271-ORD-2432. (War Pool photo ref. 30044 PME)

Below: Normandy, July 1944. An M3A1 Diamond T halftrack in a village. Drawing a 57-mm cannon, this vehicle with registration no. USA-W-40662629 also belongs to order no. W-271-ORD-2432. (U.S. Army Signal Corps)

Above: Sartilly near Avranches, Normandy, July 1944. A column of German prisoners alongside the columns of U.S. troops and equipment moving up to the front. The crews of the M5 light tank and the Diamond T halftrack (USA-W-4063352) look on. (U.S. Army SC-144994)

Left: Aberdeen Proving Ground, June 23, 1943, administrative presentation of an M3 after it has been converted to an M3A1. Coming from contract no. W-271-ORD-1023, its registration no. USA-40102943 does indeed designate it as being a Diamond T and a former M3 personnel carrier. (U.S. Army ORD-86666)

of production, with the M3 staying in production until September; it was replaced on the production lines only in October. The Diamond T Motor Car Co. supplied the Army with 3,413 examples of the M3A1, of which 845 were assembled in the factory with a crossing roller on the front and 2,568 with a standard winch.

M3s become M3A1s and M3A2s

Though the M3A1 personnel carrier became the production standard, the thousands of M3s built were not mothballed. In the case of the 7,410 examples built by Diamond T and supplied to the U.S. Army, 2,289 were converted to M3A1s. Selected companies were given the job of converting and improving them. The program was vast with all worn parts being replaced, with new tires, new tracks, and new engines being a standard exchange. Wylie Inc. brought 844 M3s up to the standards of the T-13146 and T-19179 contracts,

Left: This former M3 from Diamond T converted to an M3A1 is easily identifiable by its registration number USA-40102907. The headlamps leave no doubt as to the vehicle's former identity. (Bippa photo ref: EA-31987)

Below: A column moving up toward Namur, Belgium, September 5, 1944. Almost obscured, the registration number designates the vehicle as a former M3 personnel carrier. (U.S. Army SC-193853)

Creating a new halftrack model came from the wish to rationalize the materiel as much as possible. International Harvester's production apart, the idea was to evolve from four models—M2, M2A1, M3, and M3A1—to just one, designated M3A2. With its registration number 40102912 attributed to the Diamond T Motor Car Co., in contract W-271-ORD-1023, this former M3 personnel carrier became an M3A2. (U.S. Army ORD-86661)

and Bowen & McLaughlin 1,045 others (the T-13426 contract). These 2,289 new M3A1s were incorporated directly into the unit fleets.

Visually, it was almost impossible to distinguish a factory-made M3A1 from a converted M3 for those with headlights on the wings behind their small protective grilles. The registration number was unchanged and enabled the vehicle to be identified.

In January 1943 a study was conducted to look at standardizing all M2, M2A1, M3, and M3A1 models into one vehicle. The aim was to regroup all the various functions of the four vehicles. Even though the program was carried out at International Harvester, the Diamond T M3 personnel carriers were used as guinea pigs. The project was designated Halftrack Universal Carrier T-29 before being renamed the Halftrack Universal Carrier M3A2 (or M3A2 universal halftrack carrier). However, in March 1944, when the project was ready for production, it was suddenly abandoned.

The T-29, or M3A2 universal carrier had a firing position for the .50-cal machine gun, rear racks, standardized external storage for mines and a specific electrical installation as well as an aerial mount for a radio. The most noticeable particularity of these M3A2s was the horizontal ladder-like structure on the body sides that replaced the tarpaulin fixation points and allowed equipment to be attached without restriction. (U.S. Army ORD-86660)

This flag proclaims:

"Well done, Diamond T men!"

BY THOUSANDS, powerful DIAMOND T military vehicles are rolling in unending columns into service—delivered "per schedule and per specification." The men who created America's first and only Hundred Thousand Mile Truck are exceeding the heavy war responsibilities our company has shouldered. They're turning out these huge army vehicles in greater volume than the normal heavy truck production of the entire industry!

The prized Army-Navy "E" banner which floats above the Diamond T factory, symbolizes the official "well done" of the nation's armed forces for the production performance of DIAMOND T men. And as proudly as a soldier's hard-won chevrons, the bright "E" badges gleam on coat lapels and overalls.

These sure skills that now serve our nation in her need, will one day serve you in peaceful commerce again. They'll be sharpened razor-keen by the long grind of war. They'll serve you better than ever. But meanwhile . . .

It's by the measure of what we do toward Victory today, that we'll deserve tomorrow's Liberty—its rights, its privileges and its responsibilities. That goes for all of us.

DIAMOND T MOTOR CAR COMPANY • CHICAGO

Buy U. S. War Bonds — For All You're Worth — For All You Cherish

DIAMOND T TRUCKS

Right: September/October 1943, these four M3A2 universal carriers are being transferred to Fort Knox on an equipment train for evaluation before a decision on their future. Once the tarpaulin was in place, the utility of the new side structure became apparent. It was no longer a question of having to use the fixed grommets on the bodywork, since the upper bar was used along its whole length. (U.S. Army Signal Corps)

Gun Motor Carriage T48

These T48 halftracks were unique in their kind. Some 963 examples were built, including the prototype; they never served in the U.S. Army and Diamond T was the only builder.

On April 15, 1942, the project to mount the 57-mm antitank gun on a halftrack was launched. The technicians at the Aberdeen Proving Ground were given the job of converting an M3 personnel carrier to a T48 gun motor carriage.

At this stage of the development, it was the British version of the gun (the Mark III 6-pounder) which was used, mounted on a tubular carriage and inside an imposing casemate.

In order to render the gun operational, the windshield with its armor and the upper structure of the body were removed with initial trials taking place in June 1942. Redesigning the vehicle began quickly,

Below: The first version of the T48 gun motor carriage during shooting trials at the Aberdeen Proving Ground on June 16, 1942. The wooden structures at the four corners of the vehicle were used to measure how far the vehicle recoiled. To facilitate the vehicle design, even the armored doors were removed. (U.S. Army ref ORD-65508)

in August; the carriage was modified to give it a more conical shape and the casemate was replaced by a more appropriate shield, with the gunners still being enclosed. With this new design, the gun could traverse 27.5° to the left and right, with an elevation of between −5° and +15°.

When development ended, the pilot model of the T48 gun motor carriage was fitted with a light windshield in two removable parts between which the gun barrel passed when in the travel position; it was secured on the muzzle lock fitted to the horizontal part of the bodywork, just between the split hoods.

Armor placed horizontally and hinged at the bottom ensured both the driver and co-driver were protected.

There was only one order for this model of vehicle: some 962 ordered as contract W-721-ORD-1023 with

Above: With registration no. USA-4019249, it was an M3 personnel carrier halftrack made by Autocar that was used as a basis for the conversion. It was Diamond T, however, that was given the overall order for this type of vehicle. (U.S. Army ref ORD-65509)

Right: Seen from the front, it is easier to understand why the windshield had to be removed, to allow the gun to traverse. (U.S. Army ref ORD-65513)

Left and below left: Recognizable by its headlamps, this is an M3 from the end of production that served as the basis for the final development of the T48 gun motor carriage. This is what the 962 examples in the production series looked like. (U.S. Army ref ORD-63389 & 68393)

Left: This view of the driving position gives an idea of how the windshield has been converted and especially how the gun barrel and the front part of the carriage take up so much space. The vehicle's overall layout leaves little room for equipment and the racks for personal weapons have disappeared. (U.S. Army ref ORD-68394)

Right: The combat position along the rear armor plating was fitted with the two 30-gallon fuel tanks and the rack for the 57-mm gun ammunition. The space available allowed for three of the five-man crew to be accommodated; the other two sat in the driving cabin. (U.S. Army ref ORD-68383)

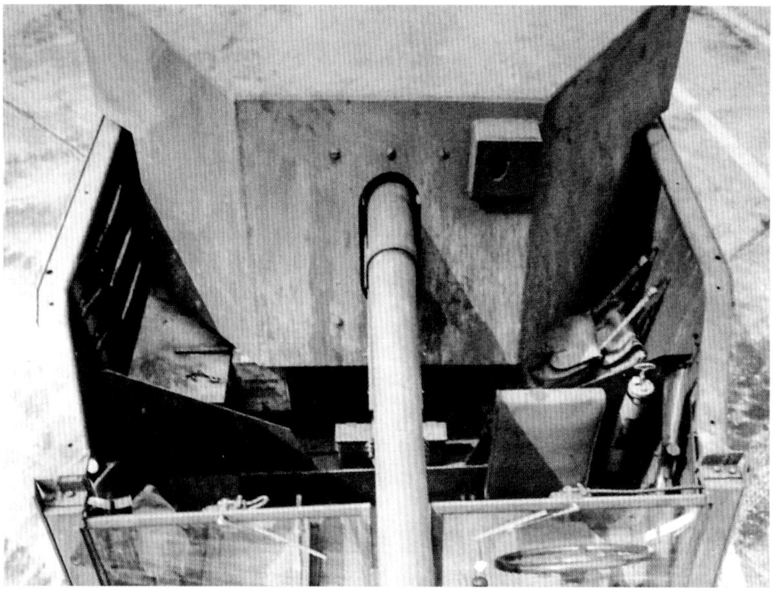

the registration numbers between USA-4029934 and USA-4021614. The UK took 30 on charge and Russia 651; the remaining 281 were transferred directly to the Chester Tank Depot to become M3A1 personnel carriers.

Above: The travel position of the barrel was secured by a barrel lock located just in front of the armor plate, which had to be left in front of the windshield. This configuration, unlike other halftracks, was used in the gun or howitzer motor carriage configuration, either 57-, 75-, or 105-mm. Only the T48 was equipped with this barrel cradle system. (U.S. Army ref ORD-38381 & 68382)

Left: The T48 gun motor carriage was considered a short- and medium-range antitank weapon. As such, the servers' protective casemate provided as much protection as possible from small-arms fire and shrapnel. (U.S. Army ref ORD-68386)

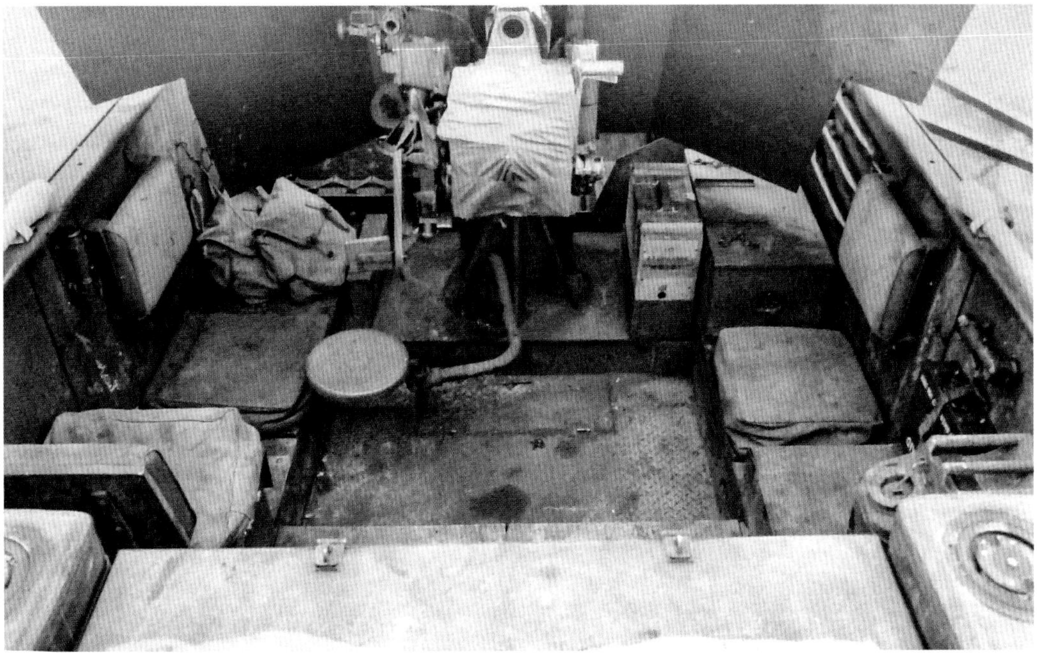

Above: The protection provided by the shield was all the more important because setting up the gun in battery meant that the armor plate had to be lowered for the barrel to traverse. (U.S. Army ref ORD-68385)

Below: Unlike the prototype, the production series vehicles were delivered with a winch and the M1 antitank gun which was the U.S. version of the British 6-pounder. Romania, August 1944, with the French 4e Régiment de Fusiliers Motorisés of the 6e Armée Blindée. (Press Agency)

Above: The T48 gun motor carriage in the Red Army. In Russian nomenclature, the T48 became the SU-57, for Samokhodnaya Ustanovka 57. (Press Agency)

Howitzer Motor Carriage T19

The T19 self-propelled howitzer was also one of a kind. Some 325 were built, including the prototype; they were used only for a short while and were only built by Diamond T.

In September 1941 the project for installing a 105-mm howitzer on a halftrack began, also at the Aberdeen Proving Ground. An M3 personnel carrier halftrack

Right: Aberdeen Proving Ground, November 29, 1941, was the first official appearance of Howitzer Motor Carriage T19. To carry out the conversion, all the structure above the driver's position was removed as was the windshield and its armor. (U.S. Army ref ORD-53813)

Left: The front of this prototype from the start of development. Anything that could get in the way has been removed; the gun's shield has not as yet been fitted. (U.S. Army ref ORD-53812)

Below: A casemate was tested before a shield was fitted onto the gun, but it overly reduced the sideways movement and the project was quickly abandoned. (U.S. Army ref ORD-)

Left: The version that was finally chosen had a simple shield with its upper sections mounted on hinges, which only provided protection from small-arms fire. (U.S. Army ref ORD-64494)

Above left: The T19 was normally used in a stationary position. The gun shield has a large indentation to allow the driver to handle the vehicle without preventing the gun from rotating. (U.S. Army ref ORD-59868)

Above right: The gun took up a lot of space in the combat position and left little space for the crew and their equipment. (U.S. Army ref ORD-64493)

Right: The crew of the HMC T19 comprised eight men: gun commander, driver, gun aimer, gunner, loader, and three assistants who managed the supplies and ammunition. There was little space for them inside the vehicle and there was none for individual equipment. Personnel had to use a backup vehicle to transport their equipment and the ammunition stock. (U.S. Army SC-169439)

With the gun set up in battery, only four men were inside the vehicle for aiming, loading, and firing; the rest of the crew were responsible for target ranging and supplying the gun ammunition. (U.S. Army SC-150506)

was used as the basis for conversion to a Howitzer Motor Carriage T19 (or T19 howitzer motor carriage).

In the first stage of the development, the M2A1 105-mm howitzer was installed inside the vehicle without a protective shield. To ensure the gun was operational, the windscreen and its armor were removed as was the upper structure of the body. Initial trials took place in November 1941 where a small protective shield was very quickly installed. It was not until March 1942 that the definitive design was finalized.

The T19's supply and support vehicle was an M3 personnel carrier, with a crew of four, that transported the equipment and the 105-mm howitzer ammunition. (U.S. Army Signal Corps)

Above: Louisville, Kentucky, April 6, 1942, a unit of Field Artillery takes part in a memorial parade. Coming from Fort Knox, the 105-mm T19 howitzer motor carriages have all the armored shutters in position, including the one in front of the driver. (U.S. Army SC-150320)

Below: October 31, 1942, Battery A of the 59th Field Artillery Battalion is ready for inspection. In the foreground, are the six T19 howitzer motor carriages, followed by six support M3 personnel carriers. At the end of the line are four other M3s used by the topographical teams tasked with regulating the shooting. (U.S. Army SC-150320)

In its new iteration, the gun could traverse 20° to the left and right, with an elevation of between –5° and +35°. At the end of the evaluation process, safety for the driver and co-driver was furnished by horizontal front armor hinged at the bottom. There was only one order for this model: 324 vehicles bought as contract W-741-ORD-6289 with registration numbers between USA-403377 and USA-403698.

The operational career of the T19 howitzer motor carriage was relatively short as the M7 howitzer motor carriage based on the M3 medium tank was preferred, followed by the Model M7B1 based on the M4 medium tank. The T19 did, however, see combat in North Africa and the South of France.

Rabat, Morocco, December 20, 1942. U.S. troops in a victory parade just four days after the culmination of Operation *Torch*. (U.S. Army SC-172540)

Above: The battle of Kasserine Pass, near the Tunisian town of Sened, was truly a baptism of fire for the Americans confronted by the Panzerarmee Afrika. The T19 howitzer motor carriages paid a heavy price, their armor unable to resist enemy artillery and tank fire. (U.S. Army SC-179251)

Below: Not many T19s landed in Europe. They initially took part in Operation *Dragoon*, the invasion of the South of France, like this example in August 1944. (U.S. Army Signal Corps)

Diamond T 105 mm. "tank-destroyers" at the recapture of Sened oasis in Tunisia—a painting based on photographs officially released by the War Dept.

"The Guns that Go Anywhere" depend on Diamond T stamina!

CANNON-CARRIER, man-mover, trail-blazer, the amazing Half-Track is proving one of the most versatile weapons of this war. As shown in the picture, the mobile howitzer is a form of "tank-destroyer" that has brought consternation to the blitz-battlers of the Axis.

It is only one of Diamond T's contributions to the fighting power of our armed forces. As prime mover, wrecker and cargo carrier, the 4-ton six-wheel-drive Diamond T is on active duty at every major front. And giant Diamond T "tank-recovery" units are shuttling shell-torn General Shermans to repair bases to be returned to battle with front-line performance renewed.

The "production-front" is delivering the goods. The E flag above our plant signifies excellence of product, and it applies to Diamond T production volume which is greater than the normal peace-time heavy-truck output of the entire industry.

A brilliant engineering staff and a redoubled production machine are devoted today to the winning of the war; when Victory has brought peace, they will celebrate with new and finer commercial trucks to carry even higher the splendid traditions of the famous Diamond T Super-Service line.

DIAMOND T MOTOR CAR COMPANY, CHICAGO
Established 1905

★ DIAMOND T MOTOR TRUCKS ★

13 Prime Mover Trucks

Designated as the Model 980 or 981 by Diamond T, or as Truck, 12-ton, 6x4 Tractor M-20 in military nomenclature, these trucks had a special role in the U.S. Army's rolling stock inventory.

Unmistakably, the creation of this lorry can be attributed to the British Army insisting on finding new suppliers, since its own national builders were overwhelmed by demand from the beginning of World War II.

As early as 1939, the British Purchasing Committee, set up in New York City, was looking for long-haul road transport vehicles able to move heavy armor. It was the Diamond T Motor Car Co. of Chicago that responded most favorably and most precisely to the invitation to tender. Contrary to the habits of the time where civilian vehicles were adapted more or less

Left: A Diamond T 980 version intended for the British Army, distinguishable from the American version only by the electrical system for the headlights. (U.S. Army SC-145071)

Below: Recently off the production lines, this Diamond T 981 is from the early production series, the winch control levers being inside the cab. The fact that it was intended for road work only, despite it being fitted with tires specific to almost all U.S. vehicles, meant that the protective grilles over the headlamps could be removed. (U.S. Army Signal Corps)

Above: Desert Training Center, Camp Young, September 1942, the 302nd Ordnance Battalion is testing procedures for using the M-20 and ways of loading broken-down armor. (U.S. Army SC-145065)

Left: As soon as the tank was lined up behind the trailer then drawn toward the platform, the longitudinal guides acted as rails, ensuring that the load was properly aligned. (U.S. Army SC-145066)

The Truck, 12-ton, 6x4 Tractor M-20 is hitched up to a Trailer Tank Transporter, 45-ton, 12-Wheel M-9 resulting in the Truck-Trailer, 45-ton, Tank Transporter M-19. Here it is loaded with a Medium Tank M-3. (U.S. Army SC-145066)

for a military role, in this particular case American engineers created two new models from scratch, the Models 980 and 981. They were 6x4, diesel-engined, so-called ballasted trucks, designed for towing trailers with incorporated dollies. Initial supplies date back to 1940/1 and were allocated only to the British and Canadians. In 1942, the U.S. Army became aware of a like need for such transport vehicles.

DIAMOND T MODEL 980 AND 981 TRUCK PRODUCTION			
Qtys	**Orders**	**Registrations**	**Comments**
835	DA-W-398-QM-4	-	702 Model 980s, chassis nos. 980-0001 to 980-0702 133 Model 981s, chassis nos. 981-0001 to 981-0133 425 delivered in 1941 and 410 in 1942, all to England
1,000	DA-W-398-QM-165	-	All Model 980s, chassis nos. 980-0709 to 980-1708 460 given perhaps a registration no. USA-526399 to USA-526858 965 delivered in 1942 and 35 in 1943, all to England
677	CD-LV-332, 464, 493 and 509	-	All Model 980s, chassis nos. 980-1709 to 980-2385 All delivered in 1942, all to Canada
1,447	W-398-QM-11594	526859 to 528305	All Model 980s, chassis nos. 980-2386 to 980-3832 248 delivered in 1942, 1,163 in 1943 and 36 in 1944
0	W-398-QM-11594	528306 to 529258	953 Model 980s, chassis nos. 980-3833 to 980-4785. All transferred to orders DA-W-398-QM-4 and -165
1,746	W-271-ORD-4460	550838 to 551317	480 Model 980s, chassis nos. 980-4786 to 980-5265 All delivered in 1944
		551318 to 551503	186 Model 980s, chassis nos. 980-5266 to 980-5451, in open cab All delivered in 1944
		565021 to 565260	240 Model 981s, chassis nos. 981-0134 to 981-0373, in open cab All delivered in 1944
		5117329 to 5118168	840 Model 981s, chassis nos. 981-0374 to 981-1213, in open cab All delivered in 1944
705	W-271-ORD-11-022-285	5118169 to 5118873	All Model 981s, chassis nos. 981-1214 to 981-1918, in open cab All delivered in 1945
138	W-271-ORD-11-022-2329	5121340 to 5121477	All Model 981s, chassis nos. 981-1919 to 981-2056, in open cab All delivered in 1945 Initial order for 228 vehicles stopped after 138 units built
Of a total of 6,548 Truck, 12-ton, 6x4 Tractor M-20s built by Diamond T Motor Car Co.: 4,306 Model 980s (sheet-metal cab) 186 Model 980s (covered cab) 133 Model 981s (sheet-metal cab) 1,923 Model 981s (covered cab)			

Above: The mass of the Diamond T M-20 (considered as a road vehicle) was well balanced, enabling it to maneuver on soft ground, justifying the fact that it was fitted with all-terrain, off-road tires. (U.S. Army SC-145064)

The Truck, 12-ton, 6x4 Tractor M-20 was thus created, and associated with the Trailer-Tank Transporter, 45-ton, 12-wheel M-9, it resulted in, as a whole, the Truck-Trailer, 45-ton, Tank Transporter M-19. At the time, the trailer did not exist since Diamond T did not make this type of equipment, so it was necessary to contact other specialists. Although the British at first turned to their own domestic trailer industry, the Americans relied on firms like Fruehauf, Pointer-Willamette, Winter-Weiss, Checker, and Rogers.

Orders

Administratively it is difficult to trace the way the orders for these Diamond T Model 980 and 981s evolved, because the orders were modified so often and the status of large numbers of trucks was changed.

The speed with which World War II unfolded meant that the Allies needed to rapidly acquire a large number of vehicles. In 1941, only 460 vehicles were programmed within the Defense Aid framework, but in early 1942, no less than 1,835 units had to be supplied. To carry out this administrative tour de force, the first contract for supplying the U.S. Army (W-398-QM-11594) was reduced by 953 trucks, these being sent to the Commonwealth armies. With deliveries commencing in December 1941 and a program ending in May 1945, 5,871 Diamond T M-20s were listed on the American rolls.

Above right: This British 980 has a CAUTION LEFT-HAND DRIVE sign to notify following vehicles where the driver is seated, not on the same side as in the U.S. (IWM)

Right: The British Army was the main user of the Diamond T M-20, with some 3,493 examples being taken on charge. After going through the British ordnance system, this 981 has two-tone camouflage and a storage chest above the winch. (IWM)

Right: The M-20s were very powerful but they still had a lot of difficulty in muddy terrain. Without help, this one will not get out by itself. (IWM)

Below: The heart of the vehicle: the 14,636-cc Hercules DFXE diesel engine, rated at 201 bhp. Its American users did not like it much, as they preferred associating the Pacific M-26 with the Hall-Scott gasoline engine. (Source TM 10-1225)

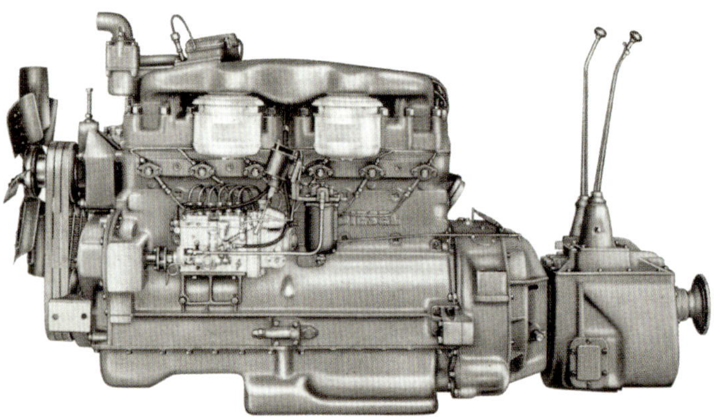

Above: On the earlier versions of the winch, the control levers were located in the cab; here the long linkage for controlling the equipment can be seen. (Source TM 10-1225)

Left: The second—the most used—version of the winch was the one where the control levers were located out on the winch mounting.

A) Clutch hand lever
B) Throttle lever
C) Drag brake band
D) Winch cable
E) Drum assembly
F) Worm gear case
G) Winch propeller shaft
H) Chain
J) Torque control assembly
K) Clutch shift yoke
L) Jaw clutch lever
M) Drag brake hand lever

(Source TM 9-768)

The accounts of supplies to the Lend-Lease program, including Defense Aid, were closed off with 4,014 Model 980 & 981s delivered to the Allies; this was almost 68.3% of the total production, of which 3,493 vehicles went to Great Britain, 471 to Russia, and 50 to France. But as nothing is ever really simple with the 980/981s, there were also three orders placed directly by the Canadian government with Diamond T without the actual numbers ever being exactly known (677 examples?). For instance, the chassis numbers 980-703 to 980-708 do not appear anywhere, leaving six non-indexed vehicles. This total production of 6,548 indexed vehicles was split into 4,492 T-980s and 2,056 T-981s.

The Differences

Be it a Model 980 or 981, there were no differences between the two trucks except for the use of the winch, the length of its cable, and certain parts like the front fender.

The 980 was equipped with a 300-feet-long cable but was only able to use it at the rear for towing broken-down tanks and loading them onto the trailer, whereas the one on the 981 was 500 feet long and could, with a set of pulleys and rollers, also be used at the front. The only two visible clues to distinguish them from each other were the front fender fitted with an opening with two guiding rollers, and the horizontal pulley to the left of the rear rollers, allowing the cable to be guided round to the front of the vehicle.

The inside of the early-production M-20 cab was cluttered with the winch controls.
1. Priming pump
2. Windshield wiper control
3. Fuel pressure
4. Dashboard lamp
5. Electric plug
6. Compressed air valve
7. Air pressure
8. Rev counter
9. Fuel gauge
10. Headlamp switch
11. Ammeter
12. Oil pressure
13. Secondary ammeter
14. Dashboard switch
15. Temperature
16. Manual throttle
17. Speedometer
18. Viscometer
19. Ignition
20. Transfer box lever
21. Main gearbox lever
22. Power-takeoff lever
23. Winch gear
24. Winch brake
25. Accelerator
26. Hand brake
27. Starter button
28. Brake
29. Clutch
30. Headlamp control
31. Engine cut switch
32. Fuel tank switch
33. Rev counter switch.

Above and below: Ordnance operation, Studebaker Proving Ground, January 29, 1945. This M-20 Model 981 with a hooded cab has reached the final stage of development. With its registration no. USA-5117370, it was part of contract no. W-271-ORD-4460 for deliveries at the end of 1944. (U.S. Army ref PGO-1910 & 1911)

Getting the cable to slip through from the rear round towards the front of the vehicle had to be done manually.

For the British Army, the 980 version was simply called tank transporter tractor, and the 981 version the recovery tank transporter tractor. Note also that for the electrical fittings, the British version had no headlamp on the front left-hand wing; the one on the right was typical of the British Army, but all the cabling was identical on both versions, even if it was not all used on those vehicles bound for Great Britain. This was only valid for vehicles supplied as part of the Cash and Carry, or Defense Aid, set-up. When it was a question of Lend-Lease supplies, the American version was delivered.

The Shape

The M-20 was a traditional truck based on a chassis with two main side members, an engine at the front, a cab behind the powerplant, a small rear body designed mainly to take 18,400 lb of ballast to ensure better traction for the rear differentials, and a central winch. This was a model 5M723B Gar Wood winch, with a nominal strength of 40,000 lb. This overall design gave the vehicle a towing power of some 115,000 lb.

Left: Like all rolling stock, the Trailer-Tank Transporter, 45-ton, 12-wheel M-9 also went through various developments born from experience. This example from early production has solid ramp triangles and only three fastening rings. The stops at the end are relatively low. (U.S. Army Signal Corps)

Left: The final development ended up with notable differences, with the front part being redesigned, the number of rings for fastening the load increasing, lights signalization fitted along the sides, and the stops at the end of the loading zone heightened. (U.S. Army SC-144971)

Below: Camp San Luis Obispo, California, 1943. With their 29½-feet length, the M-9 trailers were large items to move around. Fortunately, with technique and the help of the ramp ends, it was possible to get them to overlap. (U.S. Army SC-144971)

Above: August 7, 1944, Torigny, southeast of St Lô in the Manche Department, Normandy, the 526th Ordnance Company recovers a damaged M-5 light tank. With the help of an M-1 wrecker truck to line the tank up with the trailer, loading operations were greatly simplified. (U.S. Army SC-192481)

Below: Designed for transporting medium tanks, the M-9 trailers were not quite suitable for lower-category armor. To make up for the narrowness of the space between the two sides of the running gear, blocks were needed to reduce the distance between the two trailer ramps. The central longitudinal guides were removed to maintain the M-5 light tank's horizontal stability. (U.S. Army SC-192482)

The Mechanics

The vehicles were powered by a 14,636-cc, water-cooled Hercules DFXE diesel engine rated at 201 bhp at 1,600 rpm. It was coupled through a twin-plate dry clutch to a Fuller Model 4B86 gearbox with four forward and one reverse gears, to a Fuller Model 3A86 auxiliary transfer box with three ratios and to Timken differentials, one free-wheeling Model 27454W at the front and a Model SD462W with double reduction for the rear four wheels.

The truck brakes also worked on the trailer: these were air-brakes, the Bendix-Westinghouse Automotive Air Brake system which, fed by a three-cylinder compressor driven by the ventilator belts, stocked reserves of compressed air in two cylindrical tanks fitted within the chassis. Fixed quick connectors for the brakes were located at the rear, on either side of the towing hook. There was also a set of these connections on the front of the vehicle to allow for possible—but not recommended—maneuvers at the front with a trailer, but above all for breakdowns and twinning with another vehicle. The manual parking brake was located on the propeller shaft, just outside the transfer box.

SPECIFICATIONS OF THE COMBINED TRUCK-TRAILER, 45-TON, TANK TRANSPORTER M-19

	Truck M-20	Trailer M-9
Powerplant	Hercules DFXE 6-cylinder diesel engine 14,636 cc. rated at 201 bhp at 1,600 rpm.	–
Length	279.18 in	356.23 in
Width	101.06 in	114.07 in
Height	101.06 in	56.03 in
Wheelbase	179.11 in	187.12 in
Weight empty	26,673.73 lb	22,039.62 lb
Load	18,364.51 lb	90,080.89 lb
Weight loaded	45,038.24 lb	112,120.51 lb
Tires	12.00x20 14 ply	8.25x15
Max. speed	26 mph	–
Fuel capacity	74.98 gallons x 2	–
Range	299.94 mi	–
Average fuel Consumption	2 mpg	–
Towing capability	115,103.36 lb	–

Fuel supply was from two 75-gallon tanks located on the outside of the chassis, just behind the cab. With this quantity of fuel and 12.00x20 14-ply tires, the M-20 had an average range (all configurations included, by itself or hooked up) of 300 miles and a consumption rate of 2 mpg.

The electrical installations were particular, four 6-volt batteries, coupled up two by two (a couple in each box under the cab); the vehicle had a 24-volt starter, a generator, plus a 12-volt regulator, whereas the rest of the vehicle used 6 volts, all the main components being made by Delco-Remy.

Left: The vast amounts of materiel bound for the North African desert meant a lot of trucks were needed. In 1940, the British Army had foreseen this situation, hence the large orders placed with the U.S. The Diamond Ts showed how versatile and robust they were, as here at El Alamein. Painted the color of sand, this 980's windshield glass has also been painted, an anti-glare camouflage, leaving only a small slit for visibility. (IWM E-13935)

Modifications

Like all other vehicles in this period, the M-20 underwent a number of modifications, most of them minor. The biggest was the transfer box, now the Fuller 3A92 but with different ratios. For reasons of resilience, the engine was curbed and was now rated at 185 bhp instead of the initial 201 bhp; the winch levers were relocated, no longer inside the cab but out on the winch itself, and the bodywork with the brand's logo shape of a diamond under the radiator cap was removed. The all-metal cab changed to a tarpaulin-covered one during 1943, which gave a few more inches of space upward when transported by sea.

Right: A very British view of hitching up: a Diamond T Model 980 and 40-ton British Mk II trailer with a Churchill ARV-1 as its load. On long missions the crews adapted their mounts to be as autonomous as possible. The body has been converted to a sleeping bay, with large stocks of fuel carried, as seen here with the 44-gallon drum. (IWM)

Below: February 13, 1943, the 1st Australian Armoured Division has just received new equipment from the United States. Truck Diamond T M-20, Trailer M-9, and Medium Tank M-3 make up this column's cartage. (AWM)

Above: July 1944, in one of the numerous ordnance base repair shops set up in Europe, the equipment to be repaired is piling up, including two Diamond T 981s. Also shown is the use of the so-called "ballasted" body which was designed to take ballast and improve traction during heavy load moving. In this example rocks were used. (U.S. Army SC-192315)

Below: Hagenau, Alsace, December 28, 1944. A Diamond T 981 of the 44th Ordnance Battalion of the Seventh U.S. Army takes an M4A1 medium tank to a workshop. The odd tires were common as the front running gear suffered greatly during heavy breakdown operations and it was necessary to change them regularly. (U.S. Army SC-198851)

Among the orders placed for the U.S. Army, in mid-1942, a small series of six vehicles—very certainly those not in the inventory—was produced in order to carry out a series of precision tests which led to the building of an example with entirely armored bodywork.

Notable too were the trials for converting semi-trailer tractors by replacing the small rear body with a cradle, and trials with different engines. As none of these led to any major improvements, there was no standardization. The British were, however, interested in the American developments, took up the idea of the semi-trailer tractor for themselves, and modified some 250 M-20s in their possession.

The Trailers

The Trailer-Tank Transporter, 45-ton, 12-wheel M-9 (or M-9, 45-ton, 12-wheel tank transporter trailer) was specially designed to be drawn by the Diamond T 980s and 981s. It was of the freestanding type, made of steel and able to take loads up to 90,000 lb. Comprising a front differential forming a dolly and a double rear axle, it rested on the ground on 12 sets of 8.25x15 twin wheels. Its upper platform was fitted with two track guides, cable guides and rollers, and pulleys to enable armor to be loaded using the truck's winch.

Various blocks, pulleys, and tackle were part of its on-board equipment and were stored in the case built into the trailer structure. Its braking system

Left: Busy traffic on the Red Ball Express: the lead military units advanced quickly, resulting in dangerously extended supply lines by the end of 1944. Ordnance used all possible means to get the supplies to the front. The M-9 trailer's large surface and capabilities made it an excellent auxiliary for moving heavy and/or cumbersome loads. These trucks could return from the front loaded with damaged tanks and other vehicles. (U.S. Army Signal Corps)

Left: In the Soissons region, north of Paris, September 15, 1944. With the help of a gauge and the truck's compressor, Pvt Lester Hartley and Cpl Paul A. Herman, of the 3595th QM Truck Company, are checking the tire pressure on this M-19, 45-ton, tank transporter trailer. Note the crates of TNT loaded inside a steel cradle with no sides, just a bottom, a front, and a rear. To ensure that the trailer and the cradle are fastened solidly together, steel supports have been welded directly to the M-9 trailer platform. (U.S. Army SC-192315)

functioned with compressed air from a compressor in the engine compartment. A manual control was available to independently activate the trailer brakes during loading/unloading.

Some 6,143 examples of this M-9 trailer were taken on charge by the American Army and produced between 1941 and 1945. Production was split between 344 vehicles from the Checker company, 1,148 from Rogers, 1,192 from Pointer Willamette, 1,632 from Fruehauf, and 1,827 from Winter-Weiss.

In the context of Lend-Lease, 3,448 trailers of this type were delivered to the Allies: 2,860 to Great Britain, 531 to Russia, and 57 to France. Some 444 examples were bought directly by Canada.

Below: Although deleted by the censors, the markings on the access ramps of this M-9 are telling. The original caption indicates that this ensemble belongs to the 457th Evacuation Sector of the Services of Supply. Having suffered in earlier jobs, the right-hand ramp is being repaired by Pfcs Harold Aeschleman and James Graham, Liverpool region, October 24, 1943. (U.S. Army SC-192316)

14

Production

When trying to draw up tables of orders, supplies, and deliveries, it is generally more frustrating than anything else because the documents are so contradictory. They are also partly incomplete and generally the lists, the most extensive ones, were closed off as of August 1945.

It is known that the assembly lines were not shut down overnight one fine summer day in August 1945 and that production series already started were completed. As long as the phrase "Program Complete" does not appear in the listings of the monthly deliveries, before that month of August 1945, it means that there were still vehicles coming off the production line.

(Cont'd page 151)

Right: A lineup of Diamond T Model 968s of the 106th Field Artillery Battalion, during large-scale maneuvers in the summer of 1941. The artillery pieces have been set up in battery and the trucks lined up to recover them quickly. (Private Collection)

Below: The Ordnance depot at Ashton Court, England, March 20, 1944. Recently unloaded, these Diamond T 969A wreckers belong to contract no. W-398-QM-11509. Before being dispatched to their various units, they will be inspected one last time. (U.S. Army SC-314435)

ANNUAL DELIVERIES OF THE DIFFERENT MODELS BUILT BY DIAMOND T	1940	1941	1942	1943	1944	1945	TOTAL
Diamond T Model 967 Cargo Body SWB [2]	366	632	0	0	0	0	998
Diamond T Model 968 Cargo Body SWB	0	1,380	0	0	0	0	1,380
Diamond T Model 968 Cargo Body LWB [3] (w/o winch)	0	1	0	0	0	0	1
Diamond T Model 968A Cargo Body SWB	0	653	2,318	2,821	989	540	7,321
Diamond T Model 968A Cargo Body LWB	0	0	0	0	0	132	132
Diamond T Model 968B special Canada/ UK	0	0	203 [1]	0	0	0	203
Diamond T Model 968A bare chassis SWB	0	19	99	343	655	402	1,518
Diamond T Model 968A bare chassis LWB	0	0	0	126	250	345	721
Diamond T Model 969 Breakdown SWB	0	507	0	0	0	0	507
Diamond T Model 969A Breakdown SWB	0	149	1,994	3,023	250	497	5,913
Diamond T Model 969B special Canada/ UK	0	0	606 [1]	0	0	0	606
Diamond T Model 970 Pontoon Truck LWB	0	144	0	0	0	0	144
Diamond T Model 970A Pontoon Truck LWB	0	0	201	375	0	0	576
Diamond T Model 972 Dump SWB	0	0	0	1,410	3,137	5,375	9,922
Diamond T Model 975 special Canada	0	307	0	0	0	0	307
Diamond T Model 975A special Canada	0	811	0	0	0	0	811
Diamond T Model 980	0	292	1,623	1,198	702	0	3,815
Diamond T Model 981	0	133	0	0	1,080	843	2,056
Diamond T Model 980 special Canada	0	0	677	0	0	0	677
Halftrack M3	0	1,087	3,905	3,581	0	0	8,573
Halftrack M3A1	0	0	0	1,737	1,676	0	3,413
Gun Motor Carriage T-48	0	0	50	912	0	0	962
Howitzer Motor Carriage T19	0	0	324	0	0	0	324
Total	**366**	**6,115**	**12,000**	**15,526**	**8,739**	**8,134**	**50,880**

Notes:
1. Unconfirmed quantity. 2. SWB = short wheelbase. 3. LWB = long wheelbase.

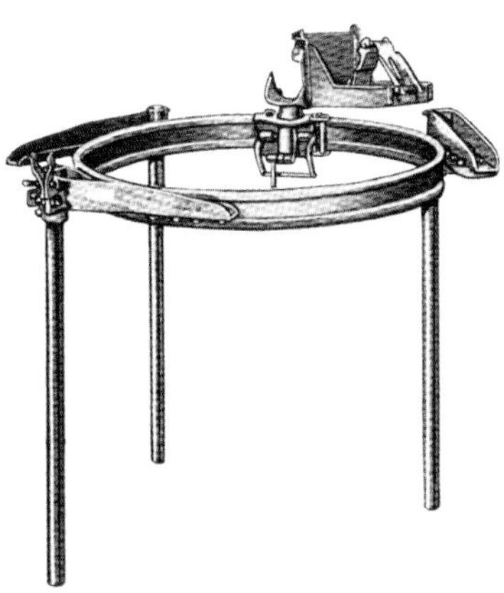

ANTIAIRCRAFT DEFENSE

Far left: It was not before the tarpaulin-covered cab appeared that the Diamond Ts were equipped with an antiaircraft defense gun carriage. This was the standard model adjustable to fit most trucks, the M-36 truck mount that was placed on three anchoring blocks installed on the cab as soon as the vehicle came off the production line. It was coupled with the M-49 ring and D40721 carriage assembly. (Source TM-9-20156)

Left: it was only after the end of the conflict when hard-top cabs became the norm that mounts other than those for the GMC CCKW appeared for fitting to closed cabs; in the case of the Diamond Ts, it was the M-56 truck mount. It consisted of a brace bolted on either side of the cab, resting on the front with a strut fixed to the cabin and to the running board. The support for the ammunition supply was also installed on the mountings but this was only postwar and concerned all truck mounts. (Source TM-9-20156)

Left: The bolted installation of the M-56 ring mount on a 968 cab. (U.S. Army Signal Corps)

Below: The telephone line construction truck for the Signal Corps, mounted on a Diamond T Model 614 chassis was nothing more than an adaptation of a civilian vehicle. Even the outline was not modified since they were supposed to operate only in the United States. (Private Collection)

(Cont'd from Page 148)

Diamond T production is mentioned in all official publications and apart from the bare chassis version where the dates are muddled, all the trucks are well documented where annual production, monthly taking on charge, and regrouping of various orders are concerned.

The only hazy point concerns the M3A1 halftrack. According to the lists there were 2,562 vehicles of this type whereas the orders suggest 3,412. This 851-unit difference can only be explained by the Ordnance Department ordering a halt since there was no M3A1 Diamond T production in 1945. Whatever the case, nothing changed much because with a production of over 50,000 vehicles in all categories for the war effort, this builder had made a fine contribution.

Particularities

As each item of information has to be sifted through and indexed, there are always oddities that are not classified. In 1941, for example, the Quartermaster Corps—at the time responsible for all rolling stock—ordered a special vehicle for testing; only one was supplied, with the registration no. USA-W-4414072. This was a long-wheelbase 968A without a winch. The basic idea for this request was to have a mix of "truck[s] with and without a winch," as with the GMC CCKW or the Dodge WC-51/52 weapons carriers, for example. In this sort of initiative, it was always a matter of cost and here the difference "with or without" failed to satisfy the Army and the project was abandoned. However, less than two years later, the idea came back into favor with the same type of mix with the 972 dump trucks.

Another oddity was the 968A cargo truck with a long 172-wheelbase chassis. At the end of 1944, two orders were placed for 607 vehicles of this type. The purpose of these trucks was not revealed, just that they were LWB cargo trucks, without designating them as ponton trucks since at the time these were obsolete. The most surprising issue was the rapidity with which 475 of these units were cancelled.

MONTHLY SUPPLY AND TAKING ON CHARGE OF DIAMOND T TRUCKS [1]

Model	968/968A & 970/970A	Bare Chassis	972	969/969A	980/981	Monthly totals
1940 Nov	50	–	–	–	–	50
Dec	316	–	–	–	–	316
1941 Jan	312	–	–	–	–	312
Feb	195	–	–	–	–	195
Mar	115	–	–	–	–	115
April	302	–	–	–	–	302
May	220	–	–	85	–	305
June	216	–	–	95	–	311
July	321	–	–	33	–	354
Aug	286	–	–	230	–	516
Sept	175	–	–	63	–	238
Oct	112	–	–	1	–	113
Nov	306	19	–	29	–	354
Dec	249	0	–	120	425	794
1942 Jan	85	12	–	240	191	528
Feb	216	16	–	156	187	575
Mar	256	0	–	99	182	537
April	241	0	–	84	162	487
May	286	0	–	95	163	544
June	203	10	–	0	169	382
July	162	32	–	47	166	407
Aug	175	3	–	198	155	531
Sept	65	15	–	201	0	281
Oct	190	0	–	246	1	437
Nov	265	8	–	335	107	715
Dec	375	3	–	293	140	811
1943 Jan	317	0	–	217	94	628
Feb	492	43	4	221	106	866
Mar	238	38	121	202	134	733
April	196	125	200	131	100	752
May [2]	144	7	188	225	101	665
June	89	0	122	341	92	644
July	132	52	200	341	100	825
Aug	224	40	180	268	112	824
Sept	212	92	273	169	99	845
Oct	250	0	122	382	102	856
Nov	357	0	0	264	84	705
Dec	545	72	0	262	74	953
1944 Jan	283	40	154	60	36	573
Feb	393	76	127	50	22	668
Mar	135	39	225	140	93	632
April	135	38	246	0	99	518
May	11	26	417	0	78	532
June	0	74	301	0	71	446
July	0	76	257	0	200	533
Aug	24	106	86	0	250	466
Sept	23	106	180	0	175	484
Oct	24	106	312	0	252	694
Nov	9	91	217	0	188	505
Dec	0	85	615	0	315	1,015
1945 Jan	50	50	720	70	175	1,065
Feb	50	50	581	57	183	921
Mar	50	49	696	85	236	1,116
April	114	124	778	70	172	1,258
May	188	39	560	70	80	937
June	88	110	889	70	0	1,157
July	50	190	784	33	0	1,057
Aug	34	135	367	42	0	578
After Aug 1945	0	42	0	0	0	42
Totals	**10,551**	**2,239**	**9,922**	**6,420**	**5,871**	**35,003** [3]

Notes to table:

1) Without taking into account building the vehicles bought by Canada and the UK, the 968A, 968B, 975, 975A, and 980.

2) During May 1943 the hooded cab was standardized on the 968As, 969As, and the 970As, as well as on the bare chassis.

3) 35,003 trucks taken on charge by the American Army: 366 units in 1940, 3,909 in 1941, 6,235 in 1942, 9,296 in 1943, 7,066 in 1944, and 8,131 in 1945.

This was more than 78% of the order, leaving only 132 trucks delivered at the beginning of 1945.

U.S.A.
20666314

USA

Additional Productions

To be absolutely complete additional productions, albeit anecdotal, cannot be ignored since they represent the effort the firm made and the reliance the Army accorded it. These orders, almost all in 1940/1, represent 309 miscellaneous vehicles:

- 3 Model 201Ss: 4x2, ½-ton cargo ammunition body version
- 136 Model 201BSs: 4x2 ½-ton bomb service M1 version
- 29 Model 404H and Ss: 4x2, 1½-ton cargo-ammunition body version
- 68 Models 614s: 4x2, 2½-ton telephone line construction versions
- 12 Model 614HDs: 4x2, 2½-ton, 40-seat passenger bus version
- 35 Model 509H and HSs: 4x2, 2½-ton cargo ammunition body and CSP version
- 26 Model 806W-DR and HSs: 4x2, 5-ton, cargo ammunition body and refrigerator versions

Or a total of 132 Cargo Truck Model 968A LWBs taken on charge (607 ordered less 475 not accepted).

Following the Ordnance Department Administrative and Tactical Vehicles Report of October 1, 1945, the following registration numbers should not have been used: 4597654 to 4597842, and 4597917 to 4598202, or 475 references withdrawn.

MODEL 968A LWB CARGO TRUCK PRODUCTION

No.	Orders	Registrations	Comments
237	W-271-ORD-11-022-240	4597606 to 4597842	Only 48 examples taken on charge in 1945 (and 475 not accepted)
186		4597917 to 4598202	Only registration numbers 4597606 to 4597653 were used
84	W-271-ORD-11-022-3739	4982404 to 4982487	All taken on charge in 1945

Opposite top: Diamond T accepted an order for 12 40-seat passenger buses. At least 10 companies made this vehicle with similar characteristics and an identical outline. This example was made by International Harvester. (U.S. Army Signal Corps)

Opposite bottom: The little bomb service M1s were the predecessors of the M6 on a Chevrolet 4x4, 1½-ton truck. Ford, GMC, and Diamond T shared the production in 1941. For the Chicago firm, this meant 136 Model 201BSs, registered from USA-W-00499 to USA-W-00541 and USA-W-001000 to USA-W-001086. (U.S. Army Signal Corps)

15

Technical Specifications

Diamond T Model 967 Cargo Truck	
Length:	268 in
Width:	9.39 in
Height:	(max) 118 in (min) 84 in
Wheelbase:	151 in
Hard-surface load weight:	16,715.45 lb
Off-road load weight:	8,357.73 lb
Weight empty:	18,066.88 lb
Number produced:	998

Diamond T Models 969 & 969A Wrecker Trucks	
Length:	283.13 in
Width:	99.5 in
Height:	116 in
Wheelbase:	151 in
Hard-surface load weight:	350.54 lb (crew)
Off-road load weight:	350.54 lb (crew)
Weight empty:	21,369.41 lb
Number produced:	6,420

Diamond T Models 968/968A Cargo Trucks	
Length:	268.38 in
Width:	96 in
Height:	(max) 118.5 in (min) 84 in
Wheelbase:	151 in
Hard-surface load weight:	16,715.45 lb
Off-road load weight:	8,357.73 lb
Weight empty:	18,066.88 lb
Number produced:	8,701

Diamond T Models 970 & 970A Pontoon Trucks	
Length:	296.37 in
Width:	96 in
Height:	(max) 116.19 in (min) 84 in
Wheelbase:	172 in
Hard-surface load weight:	16,808.05 lb
Off-road load weight:	8,007.19 lb
Weight empty:	18,516.63 lb
Number produced:	720

Diamond T Model 972 Dump Truck (without winch)	
Length:	254.5 in
Width:	94 in
Height:	113.13 in incl. cab protector
Wheelbase:	151 in
Hard-surface load weight:	17,315.11 lb
Off-road load weight:	9,208.71 lb
Weight empty:	17,215.90 lb
Number produced:	1,410

Diamond T Models 968 & 968A Chassis (Water Distribution)	
Length:	266 in
Width:	95 in
Height:	109 in
Wheelbase:	151 in
Hard-surface load weight:	7,222.34 lb
Off-road load weight:	7,222.34 lb
Weight empty:	19,301.47 lb
Number produced:	105

Diamond T Model 972 Dump Truck (with winch)	
Length:	264.63 in
Width:	94 in
Height:	113.13 in incl. cab protector
Wheelbase:	151 in
Hard-surface load weight:	16,464.12 lb
Off-road load weight:	8,355.52 lb
Weight empty:	18,066.88 lb
Number produced:	8,512

Diamond T Models 968 & 968A Chassis (Swinging Boom)	
Length:	341 in
Width:	96 in
Height:	130 in
Wheelbase:	151 in
Hard-surface load weight:	8,007.19 lb
Off-road load weight:	8,007.19 lb
Weight empty:	18,417.42 lb
Number produced:	unknown

Diamond T Models 968 & 968A Chassis (Map Reproduction)	
Length:	294 in
Width:	92.46 in
Height:	136 in
Wheelbase:	172 in
Hard-surface load weight:	4,102.80 lb
Off-road load weight:	4,102.80 lb
Weight empty:	23,020.67 lb
Number produced:	unknown

Diamond T Models 968 & 968A Chassis (Rotary Drill)	
Length:	351.47 in
Width:	94 in
Height:	136.93 in
Wheelbase:	172 in
Hard-surface load weight:	350.54 lb (crew)
Off-road load weight:	350.54 lb (crew)
Weight empty:	22,879.58 lb
Number produced:	unknown

Diamond T Models 968 & 968A Chassis (Asphalt Tank)	
Length:	266 in
Width:	96 in
Height:	108 in
Wheelbase:	151 in
Hard-surface load weight:	6,805.67 lb
Off-road load weight:	6,805.67 lb
Weight empty:	19,517.53 lb
Number produced:	177

Diamond T Models 968 & 968A Chassis (Bituminous Tank)	
Length:	328 in
Width:	96 in
Height:	107.00 in
Wheelbase:	151.00 in
Hard-surface load weight:	8,007.19 lb
Off-road load weight:	8,007.19 lb
Weight empty:	20,716.84 lb
Number produced:	285

Diamond T Models 968 & 968A Chassis (Oil Field Body)	
Length:	294 in
Width:	96 in
Height:	106.39 in
Wheelbase:	172 in
Hard-surface load weight:	16,014.38 lb
Off-road load weight:	8,007.19 lb
Weight empty:	19,537.37 lb
Number produced:	unknown

Diamond T Modified Models 968 & 968A (1,350-gallon Gasoline Tank)

Length:	268 in
Width:	96 in
Height:	104 in
Wheelbase:	151 in
Hard-surface load weight:	8,106.40 lb
Off-road load weight:	8,106.40 lb
Weight empty:	18,115.39 lb
Number produced:	unknown

Diamond T Modified Models 968 & 968A (950-gallon Gasoline Tank)

Length:	266 in
Width:	96 in
Height:	98 in
Wheelbase:	151 in
Hard-surface load weight:	5,705.56 lb
Off-road load weight:	5,705.56 lb
Weight empty:	17,614.94 lb
Number produced:	unknown

Diamond T Modified Models 968 & 968A (Sprinkler)

Length:	286 in
Width:	96 in
Height:	102 in
Wheelbase:	151 in
Hard-surface load weight:	10,809.27 lb
Off-road load weight:	10,809.27 lb
Weight empty:	20,117.18 lb
Number produced:	unknown

Diamond T Models 975 & 975A Trucks (Canada)

Length:	326 in
Width:	100 in
Height:	131 in
Wheelbase:	201 in
Hard-surface load weight:	350.54 lb (crew)
Off-road load weight:	350.54 lb (crew)
Weight empty:	27,359.37 lb
Number produced:	unknown

Bibliography

Principal Technical Manuals

TM 9-2700 Principles of Automotive Vehicles, 11/18/1947

TM 9-2800 Standard Military Motor Vehicles, 09/01/1943

TM 9-2800 Military Vehicles, 10/00/1947

TM 9-2800-1 Military Vehicles, 09/00/1953

TM 3-255 Chemical Handling and Loading Equipment, 10/30/1943

TM 3-256 Swinging Boom Crane Truck M105/25/1945

TM 5-245 Map Reproduction in the Field, 05/00/1945

TM 5-295 Water Supply and Water Purification, 05/15/1942

TM 5-297 Wells, 08/01/1957

TM 5-350 Military Pipe-Line Systems, 11/15/1943

TM 5-1134 Distributor, Bituminous Truck-Mounted, 04/00/1944

TM 5-1148 Distributor, Asphalt Truck-Mounted, 01/00/1944

TM 5-1150 Distributor, Water Truck-Mounted, 11/27/1943

TM 9-224 Machine Gun Mounts, 04/22/1943

TM 9-710-A Technical Manual Halftrack, 09/16/1942

TM 9-710 Technical Manual Halftrack, 05/00/1953

TM 9-811 Truck 4-ton, 6 x 6, 01/25/1944

TM 9-768 45-ton Tank Transporter: Truck Trailer M-19, 10/25/1944

TM 9-768 (fr.) 45-ton Tank Transporter: Truck Trailer M-19, 06/00/1954

TM 9-1768A Tractor Truck M-20- Engine, Clutch, Fuel & Cooling System, 06/22/1945

TM 9-1768C Trailer M-9, 05/25/1945

TM 9-2016 Operation and Organizational Maintenance Ring Mount, 02/21/1957

TM 10-1225 Maintenance Manual, Model 980-981, 06/10/1941

TM 10-1532 Parts List Truck 4-ton, 6 x 6, 06/00/1942

TM 10-1533 Maintenance Manual Truck 4-ton, 6 x 6, 06/00/1942

TM 10-1603 Maintenance Manual Truck 4-ton, 6 x 6, 08/16/1941

TM 10-1605 Maintenance Manual Truck 4-ton, 6 x 6, 00/00/1941

TM 10-1607 Maintenance Manual Truck 4-ton, 6 x 6, 10/07/1941

C661-DT1 Maintenance Manual 4-ton, 6 x 6, Canadian, 00/00/1941

969B-01 Parts List 4-ton, 6 x 6, Canadian, 06/00/1942

Mat-2827 6 x 6, 4-ton trucks, 06/14/1951

SNL G-159 Truck, Trailer, 45-ton, Tank Transporter M-19, 08/20/1944

SNL G-509 Truck 4-ton, 6 x 6, 12/28/1944

SNL G-509 ch.1 Truck 4-ton, 6 x 6, 03/15/1945

Other Documents

Engineering of Transport Vehicles, 1942–1945 (Chief of Ordnance-Detroit) 1945

Historic Military Vehicles Directory (B. Vanderveen) After the Battle Publications

History of United States Halftrack Vehicles (Nara)

Lend-Lease Shipments World War II (Office Chief of Finance, War Department) 12/31/1946

Official Production of the United States, July 1, 1940 to August 31, 1945. 09/01/1945

Ordnance Department, Administrative and Tactical Vehicles, 1940–1945 (Automotive Center) 10/01/1945

Ordnance Department, Administrative and Tactical Armored Vehicles, 1940–1945 (Automotive Center) 05/01/1945

Ordnance Department, Administrative and Tactical Vehicles, 1940–1944 (Automotive Center) 01/01/1944

Summary Report of Acceptances, Tank-Automotive Material, 1940–1945 (Chief of Ordnance-Detroit) 1945

The Observer's Fighting Vehicles Directory (B. Vanderveen) Frederick Warne & Co. Ltd.

US Military Wheeled Vehicles (Fred W. Crismon) Crestline Publishing

Acknowledgments

A very special thanks for their help and indefatigable support to Alexandre Delbes without whom the documentation used could not have been assembled and consulted, and Michel Roques, my long-standing friend and untiring re-reader of texts and supplier of advice of a high historical content. Thanks to the company TM-WWII PDF Military Manuals for its availability and its documents (www.-TM-ww2.com/).

Other Titles in the Casemate Illustrated Special Series:

U.S. ARMY AMBULANCES AND MEDICAL VEHICLES IN WORLD WAR II

by Didier Andres

A fully illustrated book covering all types of ambulances and medical vehicles used by the U.S. Army during World War II.

JULY 2020 | 9781612008653

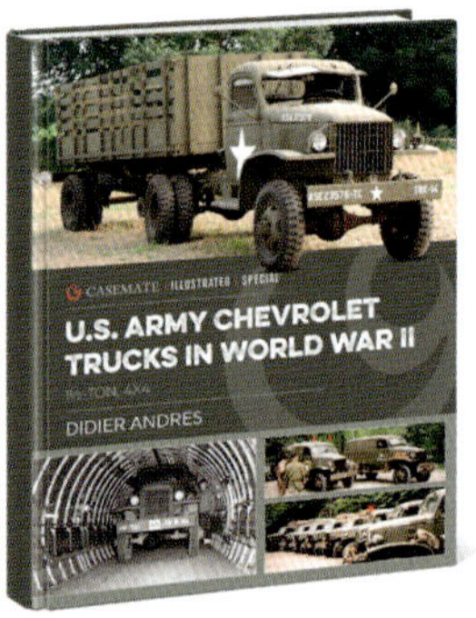

U.S. ARMY CHEVROLET TRUCKS IN WORLD WAR II

by Didier Andres

A fully illustrated and detailed account of the 1 ½-ton Chevy truck and its use by the U.S. Army during World War II.

MAY 2020 | 9781612008639

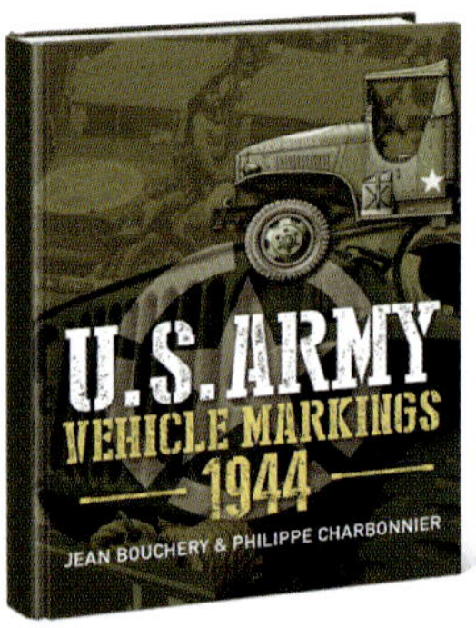

U.S. ARMY VEHICLE MARKINGS 1944

by Jean Bouchery and Philippe Charbonnier

The ultimate guide to the markings used on U.S. Army tanks, lorries and Jeeps in 1944, invaluable to historians, modelers and collectors.

JUNE 2019 | 9781612007373

U.S. ARMY SIGNAL CORPS VEHICLES 1941–45

by Didier Andres

A comprehensive and fully illustrated account of all the vehicles needed to move, use, and maintain communications equipment vital to the success of the U.S. Army during World War II.

OCTOBER 2021 | 9781636240640